WARMING FIRES
The Quest for Community in America

WARMING FIRES

The Quest for Community in America

JAMES ^Earl SELLERS

A Crossroad Book

THE SEABURY PRESS • NEW YORK

The Seabury Press
815 Second Avenue
New York, N.Y. 10017

LIBRARY OF CONGRESS CATALOGING IN PUBLICATION DATA

Sellers, James Earl.
Warming fires.

"A Crossroad book."
Includes bibliographical references.
1.   United States—Moral conditions.   2.   Social
values.   I.   Title.
HN90. M6S44   170′.202   74-28283
ISBN 0-8164-0273-6

To My Parents

CONTENTS

Preface

WALKING BACK from getting my mail at Vanderbilt, I could see a big white moving van in the apartment parking lot. BEKINS, it said in curving green letters. I did not have to ask whose furniture it had come for; it had come for mine.

"Let's go to Houston, man!" This was Jackie, the assistant, standing in the bay of the van. Frank, the driver, had already gone in to size up his cargo, my belongings.

Later Frank and Jackie unloaded my things in Houston. They put off books at Rice University and brought the furniture out to my new apartment.

"Man, you better off in Houston than Nashville," Jackie pronounced.

"Why?"

Jackie liked the help he got from bystanders on the Rice campus when he unloaded my books—"much more than back there at Vanderfleet."

"Jackie, that ain't no reason at all," Frank said.

Still, I hoped Jackie was right. I had moved before, but this time it was a bigger change. New job, teaching undergraduates at Rice—how different might that be from teaching theology students at Vandy? Recently divorced, I now had to fashion a new life, starting practically at square one, for I knew very few people in Houston.

It all added up to what I call later in this book an

initiation experience.* Jackie turned out to be right, but it took a while.

One result was to set me thinking more in personal terms about the meaning of community. The country itself, I also began to see, was going through some kind of transition, some crisis of community. This, too, was worth pondering.

What counts is that we learn from our losses and go on to reaffirm and rebuild. That is the note about America that I have tried to sound here.

I have written this book not for fellow theologians, but for fellow Americans. I have endeavored to give an honest and critical account of the ways in which we have failed at community in this country. But I have also gone on to lay out evidence that we will come through our troubles and find new community. Above all, this book expresses my feeling that the time has come to talk once again about our common hopes and possibilities. It is thus directed to all those who feel the pull, after all, of "being an American," and have the intellectual curiosity to want to rethink the promise of America for her third century, after the mixed results of the second.

I should add a word on how this book came to be written. Richard Neuhaus asked me to write an article on American community for *Worldview.* I welcomed the chance; he helped me with ideas of his own. The article appeared in the July, 1972, issue. Then Justus George Lawler of The Seabury Press suggested that the article become a book. By this time Reid Isaac had become Senior Editor of Crossroad Books. He turned out to be one of the more helpful and demanding editors that I have worked with.

I have to thank these three for eliciting from me much of what follows. But I have done it my way, and they are in no sense responsible for the flaws and

---

*Complete even with a ferryman, to "take me across" (Frank), and a seer or oracle (Jackie). See the story of Gilgamesh in Chapter IV.

liabilities. I would also like to thank three friends for critically reading the manuscript: Margaret Furse, Rosemary Minard, and Jerry Thagard. I am indebted to Ann Harrod for exchanging letters and ideas with me on the items of this book.

Because of the subject-matter and my first-person approach I have written a good deal about the lives of friends and acquaintances. Where I thought privacy should be protected I have used fictitious names and sometimes altered nonessential biographical details.

JAMES SELLERS

Technical Postscript

For readers interested in the technical aspects of theology and ethics, I offer the following observations:

1. This book is a further effort at investigation of the American moral tradition, a project begun in my *Public Ethics: American Morals and Manners* (New York: Harper & Row, 1970). There I set out to write ethics in the spirit of Montesquieu and de Tocqueville. Here I have meant to hold to this aim.

2. As to method, I have experimented with what for me are new tools. Not primarily a piece of historical or sociological work, this book is rather an essay in applied moral phenomenology, in which I have attempted the eidetic intuition of three moral essences in American culture. I have also made extensive use of mythic categories, especially initiation, as a means of exposing the intentionality of the American moral tradition.

3. As will be evident, I continue to feel that the principal subject-matter of the ethicist is morality, viz., how people treat each other, rather than theoretical paperwork, viz., what other ethicists say in books and journal articles. This latter material is invaluable, but only in the sense of helping us do our main work.

4. The most suggestive work I have come across in the reading I did for this book is *Les Contes de Perrault et les Récits Parallèles,* by P. Saintyves (pseud.), published in 1923 (Paris: Librairie Critique). It shows the mythological origins of the stories from "Mother Goose" published by Perrault. For me, it was an exciting and instructive model for interpretations of the sayings and lore of a culture. I'd like to use it some day on American comic strips. (See Chapter V below.)

J.S.

WARMING FIRES
The Quest for Community in America

I

The Death Throes

To PROMOTE its 500 Steel Belt tire, the Firestone Rubber Company took out an unusual page ad in the newsmagazines. Eight people are shown with their backs turned—eight reverse mug shots.

"We asked people if they would stop and help if you had tire trouble," runs the message. A footnote explains that data was gathered from interviews in Albany, N.Y., Atlanta, Hudson, Ohio, St. Louis, and Los Angeles.

A balding man pictured in what looks like, from a back view, an Ivy League suit, insisted that he didn't pry into other people's affairs; that seemed to include tire trouble.

A black said no: that in days gone by he had often stopped to help, but not any more.

A white youth with tapered haircut and windbreaker said he didn't like getting involved.

A teen-ager said she just wouldn't stop on the road for anyone.

The other answers were of like sort.

These responses, Firestone goes on to suggest, constitute reason enough for investing in the 500 Steel Belt, for it's a tire that "puts steel between you and tire trouble."

And then, in one of those mind-boggling reversals of modern mass advertising, Firestone gives us its nickname for the 500 Steel Belt: "the People Tire."[1] A more logical name, it would seem, might be "the un-People Tire."

Advertisers, in other words, now openly promote their products by reminding us of our apartness. A few years ago they were doing so by reminding us of our togetherness. You can count on it, the advertising themes wouldn't have shifted without good reason.

We have been aware for some time of an alleged "decline of community" in America. Teaching for twelve years in a theological school, I heard more than I wanted to hear about how bad things are. "Community is dying" became almost a cliché, a daily lament of colleagues and students. The decline was seen at every level—affecting both America at large and such smaller corporate realities as the life of our school. The sense of a common existence had lost not only its conjuring touch over space, it had contracted in time as well. Americans, by this account, now had little or no awareness of continuity or of tradition. There was no enticing vision of the future. In general, people no longer cared about each other in any larger dimensions of social or political life, and there was nothing left to do but fall back upon tiny redoubts of private affiliations, and know we were worse off.

But theological schools are still as sheltered from the world in some ways, I soon found, as Luther had said the monasteries were. Finally I left Vanderbilt and the placid, not quite "big city" life of Nashville for the undergraduate campus of Rice University and the roaring wonder of Houston, still exploding with skyscrapers, shopping centers, and big apartment projects. And at this point I began to realize that things were much worse than my colleagues and students back at Vanderbilt had been saying. They, at least, had been complaining about the loss of community and minded its demise, thinking themselves robbed of something that counted. On the larger national scene, I came to see, there is not much regret. Rather there is an acceptance of life in America without wider community.

Until recently the decline of community in America was felt and feared by many people. If the nadir wasn't here yet, some could see it coming or feel it in their bones. Still it was unfashionable, or embarrassing, or even unpatriotic to concede or even recognize the loss. It was incumbent on us to deplore it. Americans were supposed to "believe" in their communities, whatever the level—neighborhood, city, the country itself. The slogans still echo in our minds: "Right or Wrong," "Hub of the Panhandle," "I AM PROUD TO BE AN . . ."

America has now, as best I can tell, moved beyond this stage of lament over the loss of community, and into a new stage, this one much more portentous, much more indicative of a crisis. There's a world of difference between experiencing a loss while not conceding it, and taking the loss and coolly making it a matter of record. This second condition is much more serious. For now we begin to lose our grip on the reality of community itself, and less and less have any means of saying what it is or what it's not. Our temptation now is to take whatever mean, shallow existence is at hand and settle for that, and even call it community. We take a tire that saves you from the indifference of other people and call it a "people" tire.

The situation, I believe, is much worse than we

realize. Community, as we have known it in this country, is genuinely in its death throes. But I also believe that community in America can be reborn, and in time for a new world that is promised in the third century of the republic. This rebirth, however, can take place only if we are fully aware of the losses we are now sustaining.

First I want to illustrate the drastic decline of community that we now experience. Later I will try to say just what community is, but that can wait until the next chapter. After that, perhaps, we can see how admitting to the depths of our plight might be just the avenue to take for relaunching of community in America. Let us start then with the situation we are in, examining the symptoms in three spheres of our life in America: the personal sphere, the "marketplace" sphere, and the national sphere.

LIFE IN THE SINGLES COMPLEX

When I moved to Houston, I asked the apartment locator service to find me something close to Rice University, so I could walk or ride a bicycle to my office. I ended up in a well-managed but very dull complex called the Bellefontaine. Here, I was within less than two miles of the campus, could make it to class in just over half an hour on foot or in less than twelve minutes on my bike, and my gas bill dwindled to the vanishing point.

What others were enjoying elsewhere whilst I was thriving on all this practicality I learned only later, when I came across Cynthia Proulx's study, published in *Saturday Review,* "Sex as Athletics in the Singles Complex."[2] In theory a study of the swinging singles situation nationally, it focused for the most part on a spectacular Houston apartment complex, Woodway Square, out in the western suburbs.

While I was riding my bike back and forth to Rice, it turns out a notable athlete of another sort emerged at Woodway Square. This hero was a 36-year-old divorced salesman, Charley Hazzard (not his real name).

Charley, it seems, had won a mating contest, a friendly sort of competition among apt males. In a year's time he had taken more girls to bed than any other entrant. His score, according to the study: 79.

Charley didn't mind commenting for the press on his relationships with these women. Given their numbers, he could have had no more than a fleeting acquaintance with some of them. But what about those he saw more often—in particular Mindy, a 26-year-old who had become his "standby"? She was the one person more or less constantly available to him in the breaks and intervals between his priapic jousts. Considering the length of time he had been seeing her, not to mention her loyalty to him, one might ask if Charley didn't after all love at least this person.

"Old Charley don't love nobody," he replied. He had tried that lifestyle of true love in his marriage.. And his wife had one day told him she never wanted to see him again. That ended love as an option in Charley's life.

But wasn't he lonely?

How can you be lonely, Charley observed, if you have your choice of women? Mindy at 26 was available any time. But there were always others, too, at any given moment. Right then, for example, Mary Ellen, at 24, was available. Jody—"I think she's even younger"—was available. So who was lonely? "I can have anything I want around here. It's just that I don't want anything."

The Charleys of America's singles suburbias, we might speculate, represent the man who cannot feel the presence of others around him. Like the classical figure of Don Juan, perhaps he cannot be sure of his own existence except by a series of endlessly repeated moments of conquest, even of reaching out. But none of the conquests is satisfying, none of the reaching out brings back the enduring and redeeming presence of another person. Thus we come to a clue worth pursuing in our reflection about "lack of community" in America: it need not be a question of lack of contacts, absence of potential partners. One may be inundated with them. There may be people in plenitude around, people we know, people we drink with, party with, talk to, and go to bed with. And so when we try to think about what the lack of community is in America, we must surely say at the level of personal life that it is not purely a question of aloneness in Robinson Crusoe's sense. While community does require the resonance of persons, we must not make the mistake of thinking that the lack of community is conversely summed up or exhausted in the idea of isolation. Aloneness, in fact, may be a partial good, a valid counterpoint, at times, to the larger good of community. Aloneness need not be loneliness.

There is, on the other hand, a powerful style of loneliness in modern America that does grow out of isolation, of not-knowing-the-others—even though there are others aplenty around us. Back at my own less exciting apartment complex, it is this version of alienation that seems predominant. Whereas at Woodway Square, there are parties, a bar, numerous swimming pools, and organized recreation, at the Bellefontaine there is little or no social life, though you can get your leaky faucet fixed within the hour.

My first friend at the Bellefontaine, Monique, materialized not at a poolside party, but in her little Fiat that wouldn't start one day. She asked me for help because I was the nearest person in sight. I confess it was a year before I got acquainted with Greene, my next-door neighbor, and then the meeting was accidental. The electric power failed one summer afternoon.

Greene had gone to sit on a nearby ledge. I rolled up on my bike, ready to start dinner.

"We got no lights, neighbor," he called. "Come have a Schlitz." He told me about coming to Houston thirty-five years before, an illiterate black of 17 from the red clay farmlands of northern Louisiana. Now he was head waiter of a fashionable River Oaks country club and owned two cars.

For every Monique or Greene I get to know, there are scores who go and come without me. I may recognize them mostly by the kind of car they drive. When they move away, they go quickly and silently. Like the couple from India just to my right as I go out my door. Young man in white coat (medical center?), fat baby, mother in sari, red dot painted over her eyes. I speak. They speak. We go no further. One morning—zap, an empty apartment, the drapes drawn back to show bare green carpet, the clean-up crew on its way in. There was the crippled girl with the dachshund in the apartment around the corner. Undaunted by the aloofness of the Bellefontaine denizens, she asked for help and got it. "Would you mind taking my laundry down to the laundry room?" I was glad to do so and made small talk with her, volunteered to help again. But then one day—no zap this time—I just realized that she hadn't been there for some time. Sure enough, a black schoolteacher now lived in the apartment.

Adding to the anonymity, strangely, is the fact that some are so young. So young they haven't emerged yet. How can that couple two doors down be more than playing dollhouse? Yet they're married, he works, she works, and they have a child—all the cares of the great American jackpot already upon them, though they strike me as infants, with unwrinkled brows. The wife, skewedly blessed with baby fat here and skinniness there, no experience, no mileage showing in her eyes yet; the husband, a thick-haired youth, innocent eyes, a smile that one day will turn cynical. But I don't know them. And they, too, will be gone for good one day soon.

Of the two situations—the heavy interaction at Woodway Square, and the wary isolation of Bellefontaine—the former is more deceptive. Neither of us experiences, I am convinced, what destiny or imagination discloses as the fullness of community. But at Bellefontaine the pain of isolation is more or less there to be seen. At Woodway Square, a coverup goes on; the Charleys and the Mary Ellens and the Jodys are keeping that painfulness at arm's length.

Perhaps, it could be argued, these are atypical examples. The heart of America is found not in its apartment projects but in its privately owned homes. That may well be: we should certainly look there. But what we will find, I suggest, is only further evidence of decline of community.

The illusion that Americans are gregarious backslappers is probably countered best of all by what we see in the precincts of homeowning suburbia. The American home is now, and has been for a long time, a well-defended territorial imperative. It is no mere slogan to say that one's home is his castle: some are nowadays built to look it. On Mauna Loa Lane in the Rolling Fork development of Houston, for example, is a model home called "The Castle." It has a heavy stone turret, a massive crenelated wall with parapets, and half-timbered roof. Briar Village, twenty-eight minutes from downtown, has a model called "Medieval Castle" (3 bedrooms, 2½ baths, "claim your share of the 'American Dream.'")

And architecture only mirrors attitudes espoused by old and young alike. A Nashville couple interviewed on their seventy-third wedding anniversary testified to the long-standing rootage of this outlook. They attributed the secret of their long, happy, stable life to the maxim: "Live to yourself."

"We like our home," said the spry wife. "We're proud of this place—ain't no reason to be ashamed of it. We've lived here for 65 years."

But, she went on, "we don't want nobody living with us. That's the way it's always been."

When they got started, they lived in a one-room cabin. There was no living room—it was more important to have places to sleep and eat. "We had two knives and two forks—we didn't expect any company—we didn't want any."[3]

The temper of our times is to increase, if anything, the fortress-like concept of the suburban home. Until I moved to Houston I served as treasurer of a small investment club. In the first years of our venture, during the 1960's, we put most of our money into "optimism" and "happiness" stocks—electronics, drugs, bowling alley machines, speedboats. These were companies that were going to ride on the wave of a cheerful American future.

By the time of the last discussion before I left the club the subject had radically shifted. We were now thinking of putting our money into burglar alarms and security systems for suburban homes.

For good or ill, the acceptance in suburbia of non-community is now so pervasive that the Sunday magazine sections print how-to-do-it articles on the subject of minding your own business. A recent "test yourself" quiz on how to be a good neighbor gave these as correct answers:

1. You shouldn't rush up and offer to help a new neighbor unpack.

2. Don't spend too much time in your neighbor's house; if you know his floor plan well, that is a sign you're wearing out your welcome.

3. Make sure you have your own complete assort-

ment of household tools (stepladder, hedge trimmers, saw, wrenches, hammer, etc.) so you won't have to call on your neighbor for them.

4. Don't go over there more than three times a week.[4]

There is another side to all this, of course. "Independence," for many, is a higher good than the "community" we feel is lost. A study of some three hundred widows of fifty or over in the Chicago area supports that position. Most of them preferred to live alone rather than with married children.

What reasons did these widows give for wanting to live alone? Freedom to do as one pleases. The luxury of not having to follow a schedule. The generation gap. Being one's own boss.

"I moved out of my son's house because they took too good care of me," said one woman. "They did too much. They would bring my food up to me on a tray. I want to be independent, to be useful."[5]

And there are droves of defenders of the singles lifestyle, even granted its element of loneliness and frustration. "The singles 'skindrome' is not a search," says a bearded Atlanta bachelor. "Its entire premise is to live life to the fullest."[6]

The number of women in their twenties who haven't married has increased by about a third since 1960. Today, as one anthropologist observes, "it is finally becoming possible to be both single *and* whole."

Still, what is chosen by so many may not be chosen because it is so good. A divorced California stockbroker told of the desperation of many of his friends at a 981-unit singles complex near Santa Monica. "Ralph, I can't stand this game," they say. Ralph who has lived there two years, allows that maybe he can't stand it either, "But it's the *only* game in town."[7]

However good going it alone may be, to exist defensively in the smallest, tightest circles we can draw cannot be anything other than disastrous in the long run. We are finally all victimized, whether we live in Woodway Square, the Bellefontaine, or in the splendid isolation of a ranch-style fortress. To understand the dimensions of our plight, however, we have to look beyond our personal lives. What are our chances at community in the environment of the marketplace?

A MESSAGE FROM YOUR FRIENDLY COMPUTER

Within the same thirty-day period two striking analyses of the working person's plight appeared in the press. They seemed to clash head-on.

"Too Many U.S. Workers No Longer Give a Damn," was the title of one analysis. But the other report was headed: "The Workaholics: Driven by Thirst That Can't Be Slaked."

According to the first version, the traditional "work ethic" (about which we will have more to say in the next chapter) is slowly fading out in America. Too many people nowadays, especially the young, don't want to work to get ahead. Let a person get enough money to last him for a while, and then he's ready to drop out.

Worse, workers don't find much to claim their commitments, their creative energies. Too many jobs are boring, lacking all wholeness and meaning. "People my age don't take much pride in this work," said Virginia B., 27, employed by Lockheed Aircraft to turn out blueprints. "You start something and it goes through 50 million other hands before it's completed."

A United Auto Workers official told of a strange new preference among some workers—for such lowly jobs as janitorial work. "You will find people who say they would rather work in cleanup and take a cut of 15 cents an hour than work the assembly line. At least on cleanup you have the choice of sweeping the pile in the corner or sweeping the pile by the post."[8]

According to the second analysis, however, Americans are still in danger, if anything, of working *too* hard—not just fiercely competitive executives and bosses, but workers "from all parts of the population," including housewives.

Wayne Oates, a Louisville teacher and pastoral counselor, wrote a book on this phenomenon with a pointed title: *Confessions of a Workaholic.* Having finally seen himself as one of those Americans whose thirst for work, work, and more work is never slaked, Oates went on a self-searching quest to reform his ways. But he found it difficult, because:

> The workaholic's way of life is considered in America to be at one and the same time a religious virtue, a form of patriotism, the way to win friends and influence people and the way to be healthy, wealthy and wise. Therefore, the workaholic, plagued though he be, is unlikely to change.[9]

Both of these analyses could be right on target. For each, in its own way, tells us how the world of commercial values is undermining the idea of community in America today. Undue importance, even reverence, has been fastened upon work as a basis for the "good life" in America, so much so that we are witnessing the inevitable polarities that emerge out of misplaced calls for salvation. One the one hand, there are the zealous evangelists of work—Oates' workaholics. On the other, there are the disaffected protesters against a misplaced value—the drop-outs. The workaholics and the work drop-outs each represent creative minorities with a certain prophetic message. The message is that something is wrong within the sphere of work, business, commerce, and that this malfunction is tied in some way to the "death throes" of community in America.

To point to these two minorities tells us nothing about the great mass of people in the middle, who are members of neither group. Surely most Americans today do not fit the stereotype of the man with the briefcase who works seven days a week (too much beer, too many TV sets, speedboats, and charcoal grills are sold in America to support that view); nor the stereotype of the scraggly haired young man in sandals strumming his guitar while the rest of us work (too many of us still want to be able to buy all those leisure-time goods).

If the emergence of the workaholics and the dropouts as visible minorities points to a problem, how is this problem affecting the great mass of people in the middle—workers and consumers who do their jobs but also like their days off—that is, most of us? We, the lukewarm ones, have let the marketplace remodel, reshape, and refashion the world we live in, including the whole notion of what community is. What people do to each other, when community goes, is turn each other into objects. We saw that happening at such places as Woodway Square. But in the world of the great American marketplace, loss of community is happening for precisely the opposite reason: *objects are turning themselves into people!* Or we turn them into people by falling prey to the illusion that they have become one of us.

Here is a message I received a few weeks ago:

You are to be complimented on the fine manner in which you have handled your BankAmericard account. Because of this excellent record, I have automatically increased your personal line of credit as noted on the front of the mailing folder. Should you desire a still higher limit, please contact the BankAmericard Center and tell them I recommend you highly.

Sincerely,
Your BankAmericard Computer.

Computers are so much in charge of me, my destiny, my credit rating, and my income tax, that it gives me a warm feeling to have this one, so to speak, patting me on the head. It's like having a policeman give you a good driving award instead of a ticket.

In a Chicago hospital, a computer has been programmed not only to obtain data from patients for their medical history files, it can also give bedside adjustment therapy. It is capable of interrupting with messages like this: "I can tell by your answers that you seem tense. Please relax." At other times it may inquire whether the patient is enjoying himself. A "yes" is rewarded by the computer's praise ("Good for you.") A "no" brings an "Aw, come on. Take a break and then continue."[10]

Our literature and moral philosophy have just not prepared us for this kind of world. Conventional wisdom draws a sharp distinction between material objects and the human heart. In Balzac's nineteenth-century novel, *Eugenie Grandet,* for example, the anti-hero is Eugenie's father, an avaricious wine merchant and speculator. Old Grandet is so fascinated with gold that he is prepared to let all the people around him suffer. A visitor comes to dinner. Nanon, the cook, suggests a *pot-au-feu.* Grandet reluctantly agrees. Nanon says she will have to have money to go to the meat market. "Not at all," replies Grandet. "I am going to tell Cornoiller to kill me some crows." Eugenie is singled out for especially horrendous treatment. She innocently turns over her small collection of gold to her impecunious cousin, Charles, about to set out for the Indies to seek his fortune. Grandet is enraged at her. He puts her under house arrest, keeps her on bread and water.

In Balzac's treatment of avarice, we are led to make a value judgment, between the love of gold as seen in a skinflint like Grandet, and the warmer human values of others, most of all in a trusting person like Eugenie.

This assumption of a sharp difference between material values (in Grandet's case, gold), and human, moral, or spiritual values continues into our own century. It is the subject of a great deal of reflection on the part of a very recent group, the existentialist writers. Such figures as Sartre and Camus often seem to be saying that the world of objects is the antithesis of the world of persons, that the great crime is to remake persons into objects.

This classical-existentialist view of the enmity between objects, and material values, on the one hand, and human values on the other, is inadequate for picturing the new situation in the world of the American consumer. Today the human is menaced not just by the encroachment of objects upon persons, but also by the cheerful, willing way in which we confer honorary humanity upon objects. The new American marketplace is conditioning us to treat objects as if they were human. We then take up an alliance with our "humanoid" things and let that alliance fill the void left by the loss of community.

Monique, my friend at the Bellefontaine, insists on calling her little Fiat "Josephine" and considers it —her, I should say—to be a member of the family. This is a harmless enough sport, I suppose. Still, it's worth thinking about. Monique was born on an island in the Mediterranean Sea and is now far removed, in Houston, from the members of her own family. She lives alone. More outgoing than I am, Monique knows a good many more people at the Bellefontaine than I do. Still, she is isolated. As far as I am aware, she has no really close friends. Five days a week she roars away in her Fiat to her routine job in the letters-of-credit department of a downtown bank. No wonder that she confers a degree in the humanities on her car. Josephine has her place in Monique's life in the same way that other apartment dwellers keep cats and toy dogs. But what does it mean to lavish affection upon a Fiat? Josephine is, after all, a piece of machinery. At least cats and dogs are flesh and blood.

Commercial things orient us in the same way that beacons and buoys tell a ship whether it is in safe waters. Ralph Keyes, after a cross-country trip, found it reassuring "to know that despite all our divisions, something was gluing this nation together—A&W root beer." The Seven-Eleven stores in California, comfortingly, turned out to be arranged just like those of the East. Keyes goes further: "I like Colonel Sanders. . . . Until this society does better with real human substitutes, . . ." Marshall McLuhan says somewhere that we really enjoy watching the TV commercials as much as the programs. I am sure he is right. One reason, I fear, is that we imagine ourselves among friends. Item: "The Sears Ah-Bra. It understands everything about your shape." Item: "Nice'n Easy haircolor: It lets me be me." One might say the same thing about visiting big shopping centers. There is a certain comfort about being in and out of all those stores, or in taking a shopping cart and getting lost in the aisles of smiles. Here is a world in which the distinction between the object and the human being has been lost, not just because we are ofttimes "dehumanized," but because the objects are taken in, welcomed, and made a substitute both for nature and for other persons.

And yet, the world of the marketplace is deadly deceptive in what it can finally offer. To venture very far into this world, to trust too much to it, is like swimming in a pool of sharks. You've been led to think you're in a community—nothing is farther from the truth.

A couple of years ago I spent the summer in San Francisco. To help finance myself, I took a cashier's check from my home bank in Tennessee to the nearest branch of Wells Fargo.

The teller referred me to the "desk." This meant lining up. When I finally worked my way to the front of the line, I found the desk presided over by an unsmiling woman who told me: "We don't know very much about out-of-state banks." Then she asked: "Do you have an account with Wells Fargo?"

"Well, no, that's the reason I had my bank in Nashville send me a cashier's check."

She turned the check over as if it might have been dragged through dirty motor oil. "Well, I don't know this cashier. Just anybody could have signed it."

"Not long ago I cashed a check like this for a much larger amount in France—"

"Well, those French, you know, until lately they were so anxious for dollar exchange."

"Yes, well thank you very much."

She said nothing. Not even "Sorry."

Much later that day, I finally cashed the check at American Express, but only because I held their credit card, and only after getting the check initialed by the nearest desk official, one Mr. Console. Between Wells Fargo, the Bank of America (where I also wasted my time), and American Express, this adventure cost me most of the middle of the day. Rule: forget about cashier's checks when traveling in California. The lack of community in the marketplace is covered over by our penchant for humanizing the impersonal, and for seeing friends where there are in fact only computers, calculators, and Fiats.

THE LOSS OF NATIONAL FOCUS

Beyond the personal sphere, beyond the commercial sphere, is the *national* sphere. This country has thrived on and has derived its essence since at least the middle of the nineteenth century from a national consensus. The American consensus owes more to the frontier than to any other single factor. It was on the frontier, far from the local loyalties and settled communities left behind, that our forefathers discovered their common stake in the *national* character of the United States of America. It was during frontier days, I believe, not in the earlier colonial period, nor in the later industrial surge, that the normative meaning of "being an American" emerged.

In our own day, however, the basis for a sense of national community has become questionable. The older pride in "being an American" has been submerged by the frustrating wars in Southeast Asia; by the underachievement of the civil rights movement of the 1960's; and by tragic failures of political leadership that climaxed in the 1970's with the exploding sensation of the Watergate scandals. We feel a sense of loss, even a nausea, as the concrete evidence mounts that the spiritual fabric of the nation is rapidly unraveling.

We do not take the franchise as seriously nowadays. After two world wars and two Asian wars, we should be more aware of our responsibilities as citizens and world-participants. But not so. Our less literate, more backward ancestors of the frontier era took the responsibility to vote much more seriously. In a study for the *Christian Science Monitor*, Richard L. Strout examined voting records of American citizens from 1840 to 1972. Before the turn of the century, he found, voter turnouts in the United States averaged close to eighty percent. After 1900 there is an undeniable, although erratic, decline. Only once between 1840 and 1890, Strout points out, did fewer than 70 per cent of American voters cast their ballots; that was in 1852, when the percentage dropped to 69.6. But in the twentieth century so far, not once has the proportion risen as high as two-thirds. In the

1972 presidential election, approximately sixty-eight million registered voters, almost half of those eligible, didn't vote. Voter turnouts for other countries—91 percent in West Germany, 74 percent in Canada, 71 percent in Great Britain—make nonparticipation in voting seem an especially American problem.[11]

What explains this shrunken representation at the polling booths in America? I believe it is another symptom of the disease that I have been calling "loss of community." It is significant that the voter turnout in America was much higher in the years of the fixing of the "frontier" tradition than it is now. Perhaps something real has gone and our sense of loss is not mere romanticism. Almost unnoticed, community in America has been lost, replaced by a spirit of factionalism. Being set over against one another has come to seem the natural order of things, even among the best-intentioned of us.

I found myself one Sunday morning at 9:40 standing around, holding a paper cup of coffee in the "Cloisters Class" at St. Godfrey's, a large church almost within walking distance of my apartment. I was introduced to Bill and Edna and Maybelle and others—a group ranging, I took it, from the late twenties right on up to the sixties. John Short, the teacher, was able, critical, and interesting. I had known him slightly through his brother, an administrator at Vanderbilt and an old friend. Short talked about the roots of social disorder in America. He implied that more concern from middle-class citizens—meaning us, his audience—might help.

During the lively discussion that followed I was surprised at the number of people who got up and said, in effect, that it wasn't their problem. Some seemed to be blaming everything on blacks, Chicanos, and students—anybody but themselves. If this almost casual reaction was any sign of what's happening to us in

America today, we are indeed a divided nation, and
some of us are quite blind to our own complicity in the
division. We have forgotten what it means to be in it
together, as Americans.

This amnesia is not limited to middle Americans,
however. Let us consider my own students at Rice.
Seven or eight of us were sitting on the patio at the
student center one steamy day, a discussion group
spun-off from my "Ethics and the Life Cycle" course.
Our assignment that day was to try to get hold of the
moral dimensions of the word "responsibility." The disastrous prison revolt at Attica, New York, was fresh on
our minds. I asked whether a contemporary in American society should consider himself in any way "responsible" for that riot and the subsequent loss of life.

"Of course," came the quick response: one is account-
able for anything that he can do something about. While
one can do more about the conditions surrounding his
own personal life and the lives of his closest associates,
still there is conceivably something he can do about
prison reform—through the electoral process, for example, now that eighteen-year-olds vote.

What about tragedies not so recent? "Do you feel any
responsibility for genocide in Nazi Germany?" Most felt
not. A Jewish student expressed concern, with some
passion, that we not let such matters reoccur, and I
grant that is accepting responsibility of a sort—but
again, limited to what we can *do something about.* This
view also holds that no young person living today need,
by any stretch of conscience, feel himself responsible for
past injustices and atrocities.

The subject turned to racial injustice. "Do you feel
any responsibility for slavery or the failures of Reconstruction?" A unanimous "no"—the one black in the
course belonged to another discussion group—with the
pallid addendum: "Of course, we should do something
about racial injustice *today.*"

Has today's injustice no rootage in yesterday, and has yesterday no kinship with us? I argued that a larger view of responsibility might assume more commonalty with both the victims of the past—and with the perpetrators. It might well include a relationship to people out of our power to change as well as to those within it; it might have to do with a common condition, rather than simply with things we can do something about. The American heritage itself might bind us not only to each other, but also in common responsibility to the rest of mankind. The students found this talk partly incomprehensible, and to the extent that it wasn't, somewhat offensive.

"What do you mean by America, anyway?" asked a bright pre-medical student, suspiciously. "I share your concern for injustice, but what is this 'people' you're talking about? You seem to think of 'America' as an entity of some kind, as a 'going concern.'" His eyes narrowed inquisitorially. "Do you?"

"Well, I suppose I do."

"Man, that shows the generation gap. I can't even imagine what this thing is you're trying to describe, 'being a good American.'"

"But what does 'community' mean to you?"

"It means my friends."

"You said you opposed injustice—"

"What does that have to do with saluting?"

This was the Thursday 1 P.M. group—a collection of functionalists, who were going to be medical doctors and engineers and geologists. I brought up the question with the 7 P.M. group—a smaller parcel of nonpragmatic night people. They agreed down the line with the functionalists. You certainly aren't responsible for someone else's past. And you aren't going to find much, if anything, at the societal or national level that could be called community.

"What is community, then?" I asked.

"It's us right here, on Thursday night." They generated a plan for a class party, an expedition to a Greek taverna on the ship channel. What if most members of the class itself—those in the other discussion groups—didn't want to spend the money? "Screw the class—we'll go without them."

At the end of the semester, the group fell apart.

Although we have found that the loss of community-sense in America affects all ages, perhaps it is the young who are most fatefully infected. Is it purely a coincidence that suicide recently has been rising as a cause of death among youth? According to some studies, it now ranks second—next to accidental deaths—among those from age 15 to age 25. Interviews with youths who have attempted, and failed, to kill themselves point to several motives, some of which are virtual paraphrases of the symptoms we have been describing under the heading "lack of community." These motives include depression, stress, isolation, inability to communicate, and the lack of availability of someone to trust and admire.

"When I get upset," one girl recalled after her suicide attempt, "I think of all the things that have happened to me, that nobody really cares, and if I went, that nobody would miss me . . ."

This feeling is widespread in America. "Any large city not showing a marked increase in young suicides is probably not recording accurately," was the comment of Dr. Michael L. Peck, a Los Angeles clinical psychologist.

What if, by some kind of widespread malaise, the country as a whole were to be swept up into this despair about itself? The signs of demise that we have been discussing long antedate the Watergate political scandals that erupted following the 1972 presidential election. But the further corruption of American ideals that occurred in that messy, blighting chapter of our history did, for some Americans, seem to tip the balance finally toward despair and resignation. People interviewed on the streets during the televised Senate committee hearings said a variety of things. Asked what the scandal meant, a New York jewelry saleswoman, 69, replied:

It means almost complete destruction of all the ideals I've ever had in the United States and in the presidency. I am destroyed by it. I'm still of the old school, and I'm still 100 per cent for the American flag and all that it stands for. It has destroyed my image completely. A woman of my age, particularly, it makes me feel that now everything has fallen down completely. We have nothing to look forward to.[13]

This woman's keen sense of loss is a sign and symptom of "the death throes" we are experiencing as a nation. But what, exactly, have we lost that makes a lover of the country despair? That is the question we will seek to answer in the next chapter.

II

What Might Be Lost

An evening with the Packers left me reeling. They're a large, close-knit Houston family, Reformed Jews, and they haven't barricaded themselves. There are eight of them in all, including the parents. They talk to each other. They touch each other—Mom thought nothing of spending half the evening sitting on the floor, bracing herself against Danny's shoulder.

There are Catholic and Protestant families, too, who experience this kind of closeness. But the evening's substance, for me, was much in contrast to what most of us in this country—glaciated by the Protestant work ethic—ever experience. It was an evening of uninhibited affection, mutual glances, casual acceptance of adolescent children who get unruly on occasion, demythologizing of sex, a place for every member. Candor comes easily among them. At a certain moment, the two girls leave for a youth meeting at the synagogue, carefully and openly kiss every remaining member of the family. When one of the girls is invited by a boy, later in the evening, to go to the Shamrock Cinema, she calls home—but not only to Mom and Pop. The remaining kids also consider the propriety of it; she didn't get permission until Danny, the senior child, had okayed it.

We spent the first chapter reviewing some of the symptoms of the "death throes" of community in America. By now, someone is certain to ask: what do we mean, anyway, by "community"? That's a fair question, and I commit myself to try for a clear definition. Before I get around to that, however, perhaps I can do even better. The crux of the matter can be arrived at by depicting as well as defining. And a depiction, I believe, can be furthered by a sketch of the evening I spent with the Packers. Whatever it is that they've still got, most of the rest of us, I fear, don't have—or if we do, we feel it slipping away.

The Packers, I'm certain, have been spared shipwreck and loss because they are, beyond being Texans (and not ashamed of it, mind you), also Jews. Some of whatever it is that can be summed up as their "Jewishness" has kept them together at the very time in our epic that the larger American heritage is becoming unwired —formerly wired for power mostly by the Puritan tradition and the frontier experience, and the Protestant work ethic.

Danny, a junior at Rice, was my first sample of Packerism. He showed up in one of my ethics classes, a skinny, black-haired fellow (Some Texas kids wear their hair a little too long, I thought). I noticed him when he came in, he was wearing a tattered painter's cap. "Instead of a final exam," he proposed, "let's have a beer party." I vetoed the idea.

Danny was a good student, except when distracted by a quirky blonde from San Francisco, who brought her Russian wolfhound to class. He was a left-wing, activist

Democrat (as was his mother, I was to learn later). Yet he was also a Texas buff. It was he who told me about Stelzig's (for Western hats—going on up past $100 if you wanted to spend the money), and introduced me to the essays on Texas of Larry McMurtry. I had known of McMurtry's novels, *The Last Picture Show* and *Moving On*—but who'd have thought he would also have a book of essays on the Astrodome, the relaxedness of Houston versus the uptightness of Dallas, and the mores of the Rio Grande Valley?

It was this same Danny who took me to the organic food restaurants of the Montrose area and served as translator when I parleyed after class with Hank the Zen freak, who brought incense along, was quite often, I suspected, stoned, and who recollected his five previous existences, one of which had been lived out along the dusty shores of the Dead Sea.

Danny invited me to come to dinner at his parents' house, and my part of the evening began when I pulled up to the Southwest Houston address he gave me. Outside, at the curb, there was a fellow about my age, perhaps a bit on the incipiently chubby side, talking to somebody in a pickup truck. This was, I guessed, Packer *père*. He paid me not the slightest bit of attention. Playing outside the door was a child, whom I took to be a little girl. Actually, it was Dave, the youngest son.

"Hi! Who're you looking for?" asks the girl-looking child (in a souvenir-from-Florida sailor's hat). "Is Danny here?" I ask uncertainly (the curbside fellow's ignoring of me has shaken me a bit).

"Sure he's here! Don't you see his CAR there? Come on, let's go find him."

Inside there is Danny, bashfully offering me a Pearl beer, letting me know that Hank the Zen freak (also a junior) and Judy, his thirty-one-year-old girl friend, are already there. We find them in the den, absorbed in a

TV show that Danny referred to as "Kreskin the Magnificent."

Soon Sam Packer comes in, moves to establish ties with me. He is a Rice alumnus (electrical engineering). He knows I teach ethics and doesn't have to ask what ethics is. We begin, however, to talk about insects (how to kill flies, ants, roaches, and earwigs). If any of this offends the reverence-for-life of Hank he does not show it, being preoccupied with the otherworldly proficiency of the seer Kreskin.

Sam shifts from insects to ethics, asks if ethics teachers check on English composition and spelling in the writings of their students. I assure him we do.

The two girls appear, laugh and chat, disappear upstairs. This leaves two sons yet unaccounted for. We retire to the back yard. Pop swats flies, keeping count, and talks about Southwest Conference football. I quickly detect that he doesn't care a fig for football of any kind. He talks anthropology. He has read Lionel Tiger and perceives, as best I can tell, precisely what Lionel Tiger is saying.

Finally the back door swings open and here comes a trim blonde. This is Mom. She had overslept. She makes a gesture and causes a hitherto unseen son to appear: this is Ed, about thirteen, I guessed, wearing striped overalls, a pink dress shirt, bearing a bowl of fragrantly oiled vegetables (squash, mushrooms, cucumbers).

Hank is devastated by this dish, and personally consumes at least half the vegetables in the next fifteen minutes.

We sit facing the back of the enormous house —enlarged bit by bit to accommodate one, then two, then three, four, five, six children. Mom disappears for supper preparations, reappears, takes a Pearl beer.

Pop explains Mom's cooking habits. "She always prepares eight times as much as we need." This turns out to be true. There are pounds and pounds of barbecued ribs and chicken, potato salad, home-pickled okra, home-made sauerkraut (you'd never eat the canned kind again), baked beans (with bacon, yet). It is all succulent. There are, indeed, tons left over.

The missing child, Nathan, appears amid the meal. He has returned from a day of bird hunting. The first thing I notice about him is a Texaco cap. He is also wearing hunter's khakis. He has shot several quail and doves. Mom embraces him: "You are so good to me, bringing me these birds." Nathan, considerably cooler in mien than Danny, is a student at the University of Texas in Austin. He has, incidentally, cared for Davy on earlier occasions through a day of hunting.

During the meal, various people appear, for this is no mere nuclear family. Two grandmothers, one using a walker, come in to share the table. Eventually, there are two or three cousins and one aunt and uncle; I remember a cousin-in-law from Israel who spoke accented English and led singing. Numerous non-Packer children appear, to talk and be fed. They know without being asked that they are welcome.

After dinner two of the visitors, plus Ed, the young brother in pink shirt and overalls, give us the "glad to see ya" sign (outpushed palm circling goodbye) and take off on their motorbikes.

I have been speaking of contrasts in this family's way, with its passion, its apprehension of others, its *chesed* or lovingkindness, with what often passes for family life in suburbia. What is important, I must emphasize, is the sum of these qualities, and not the *size* of the family. The same quality of life ought to be achievable in smaller human groupings. What was going on in this family? Was it a denial of the suburban motif of the fortress—or was it, paradoxically, a raising of the suburban ethos to infinity? Could I play the role, I found myself wondering, of Sam Packer? Such questions never occurred to him. He seemed completely at home with his identity. There was a big, expensive color enlargement of the whole family in the parlor. He was planning to move it to his new office the next week. He and his family were living out of some reality that they took for granted.

A DEFINITION OF COMMUNITY

Why start with the Packers? What about their family life is helpful in arriving at a definition of community? Whatever it is, it is not something that we can point to in the life of just any family. By looking at the Packers we begin our quest for a redefinition of community in a positive way, for their common life points to something that is harder and harder to find, as this recent wire service story illustrates all too well:

FAMILY LIFE
TOO IMPERSONAL

New York (UPI)—Where has love gone? that's a question asked by John L. Thomas, S.J., a Georgetown University sociologist. Father Thomas says in the family there is an increasing tendency to impersonal relations. There is a lack of affection, warmth and relaxation in the home, he says.[1]

The moral of the Packers' story is not that they have found their way *out* of the American dilemma. They share the same fate as the rest of us. If the country continues to lose its common spirit, its community, and sinks into existential death, they sink, too. "After all," as a Jewish theologian warned me, "whatever is happening to other Americans must sooner or later overtake us, too. You Protestants may be a hair's breadth ahead of the Catholics, and a generation ahead of us, in your slippage. But if it happens to you, it will happen to us. In our case, all it would take is for our kids growing up right now to lose just a little more of their 'inner hearing.' Externally, we're pretty much alike already."

I remembered one Packer boy and his motorbike and overalls, and another Packer boy and his Texaco hat and shotgun, and thought: how true.

Moreover, we must be careful about beginning with a *family's* life as a basis for constructing a definition of community. Ordinarily some broader base is sought —the life of a city or region, for example, or the common spirit of a country. Yet a valuable clue for defining community at any of these levels comes from observing the life style of the Packers. To use a figure of speech, one that I am driven back to continually, there's a "warming fire" there, still burning, whereas the fire seems sputtering out or exhausted in a great many other hearths of the American scene.

What is this warming fire? Both the Packers and Charley Hazzard, the Don Juan, champion wooer of Woodway Square represent human beings in quest of the company of other human beings. But there's a fundamental difference, it seems to me. The Packers, in their mutuality, are expressing something that already exists in their lives. The Charleys are seeking, searching, forever reaching out, for something that doesn't. "If you have to make a journey to track love down," says Harry Lesser, in Bernard Malamud's novel, *The Tenants*, "maybe you're lost to begin with. No journey will help." Let us consider the contrasting experiences brilliantly described by the philosopher Gabriel Marcel, the difference between "being" and "having," or between "being with another person," as we may paraphrase, and "having," or even "having at" another person. Community at any level, as we are going to define it here, always partakes in some way of being rather than having. Community is the outgrowth, the expression, of being-with; it is the celebration of life together.[2]

Alfred Shutz has a helpful term for this building-block of community. He calls it the "we-relation." It is the basic pattern of human activity; we presuppose it in everything we do. The we-relation is so fundamental to human experience that we have to take ourselves as social before we can even be individuals, and certainly before we can talk about ourselves as a "mass." Person-hood flowers when "I am oriented to you, and you, in turn, take my existence into account." In that situation, "a social relation becomes constituted." This is the we-experience, which "forms the basis of the individual's experience of the world in general."[3]

The surprising truth, says Schutz, is that "my partner is given to me more vividly and, in a sense, more 'directly' than I apprehend myself." After all, the other is there for me to participate with. I can know him in the course of his and my acts, our give-and-take, my questions to him, his questions to me. But if I want to know myself, I have to suspend all this live action and think about myself as I have lived my life up to here. That is reflection instead of action. It is less a living, vivid experience than the process of relating in the present moment with my fellow man.[4] The we-relation is live; self-knowing is on tape.

Thus the lived social world has a new character that outruns what either you or I or any of the others give to it individually. We all make an input. We share an environment. We jointly undergo experiences. But in the fusion of the we-relation the world takes on a new meaning given it by this "intersubjective" enterprise. "It is not my environment nor your environment nor even the two added; it is an intersubjective world within reach of our common experience."[5]

Perhaps the most crucial aspect of the we-relation is

the experience that Schutz speaks of as "growing older together" A fair test of whether our being-with-others is true community or not, is whether we do share the reality of "growing older together." The Packers are, I should say, growing older together—adding rooms to the house as more children come, learning how to make decisions in a way that encourages the children to join in, talking to each other as time goes on. Don Juan, or his swinging counterpart, the champion wooer of Woodway Square, is not growing older together with anyone; he is growing older alone. For he is not "with" his lovers as a way of celebrating an existing reality, or of warming himself at a fire burning there. On the terms of the we-experience, he is not really "with" these ostensible partners at all. They are only successive long shots, glimmering chances, usually a-going, for something sought and not yet had. And his lovers—his Mindys, Sue Ellens, and Jodys—are also growing older alone.

How little this aspect of community is recognized in America today! The we-relation is ordinarily reduced, in the sights of the mass media, to a celebration of the present. That segment of community so hopeful and dynamic until recently as the "youth revolution" entertained no notion of "growing older together." Perhaps the best example of our bemusement was the punch line for a woman's hair product drummed into our skulls in TV commercial breaks: "You're not getting older —you're getting better." The truth is, the only way one can get better is to get older. And the only way to community in America, the only way to justice and progress, is to "grow older together."

Let us sum up. In one way or another, it is the *we-relation across time* that is the essence of community. Even in larger social groupings—the life of a city or of a nation—we will find there is something at least analogous to this living, ongoing mutuality at the heart of true community—the "warming fire" which we come to and gather round. To be sure, we cannot live every dimension of our lives in the pure we-relation, or in face-to-face dealings with other persons. A friend leaves my presence; we are each of us then on his own. He becomes at that point an indirectly experienced contemporary, not a directly experienced we-partner. The relationship changes. "I know that he is in some Here and Now of his own, and I know that his Now is contemporaneous with mine, but I do not participate in it, nor do I share his Here."[6] He will have changed in some way when I see him next.

Moreover, I must constantly deal with others in ways that do not allow them to appear to me fully as persons—I must deal with them as parts of groups, as "types," as anonymous typical others. But even here, we shall find, it is a mistake to conclude that there is no longer any "mutuality," or direct, shared life. At every level of community there is a "warming fire" appropriate to that level, that is analogous to, if necessarily different from, the "we-relationship" of the personal level of community. At the national level, which is the focus of this book, for example, the proper analogy to the we-relationship used to be called "love of country," but as we have already seen, it is a warming fire that appears to have been burning itself out.

So far we have established that community, beginning at the personal level, takes on the character of a we-relation. It is a kind of "being-with" rather than a "grab-for" or an attempt to "have" or "have at." And it is realized only as we move on, progress, age, "grow older together."

Although the we-relationship or something like it is the "heart" of community as we are defining it, we now have to add two further elements.

First, the we-relation cannot exist alone, or generate itself. To put matters simply, it "comes from somewhere or something." It springs from some bedrock belief, faith, ethic, or value system. If the we-relation is the fire, this prior-something we are now discussing is the fuel that feeds the fire.

To define this prior-something will require a shift from sociological talk into ethics, and we will turn to that task in the next section of this chapter.

But there is one other component of community that we must first briefly examine. The we-relation is not only the outcome of a prior value system; it also becomes, in turn, the source of a distinctive set of institutions, and of its own ways of organizing groups.

The sociologist Robert MacIver in a helpful definition of community makes a distinction between "community" and "association." For MacIver, a community is a focus of common life. It may be a village or town. It may be a district or country. It may take in an even wider area. To earn the name of community this area or group must have something distinctive about it, something that holds it together, something that gives it, right up to its frontiers, some special meaning. (It is easy to see that this something-distinctive corresponds, in a way, to the "prior-something" I have just been talking about.) But communities are not rigidly organized into areas with sharp boundaries. They fit together, lesser communities into greater ones. Any community may be a part of a wider one, just as a local bowling club, let us say, may have an identity of its own and yet be a part of a much larger fraternity of bowlers. Thus "all community is a question of degree."

Nevertheless, a community is something definite. It is a grouping of people into a special pattern of existence. It is shaped by the nucleus of a distinctive and even intense common life. Concrete examples, says MacIver, are the city, the nation, or the tribe, which he calls "par excellence communities."

We must be careful, however, not to confuse community with the limited organizations that show up in its life. MacIver calls the limited organization an association. An association is a functional spin-off of community. It is an organization put together or used by the community. It expresses the interests or meaning of the community. "Community bubbles into associations permanent and transient," says MacIver. "A community is a *focus* of social life, the common living of social beings; an association is an *organization* of social life, definitely established for the pursuit of one or more common interests." Whereas associations express partial realities, communities are wholes. Community is prior (the "warming fire" that we have been speaking of), it is something "wider and freer" than even the greatest associations. Community is "the greater common life out of which associations rise, into which associations bring order, but which associations never completely fulfill."[7]

Thus the family, we might say, is a basic association meant to express the "we relationship." At the other end of the scale, we encounter the most powerful association of all, the state. It is crucial to our understanding of American community to see that the state itself is *not* community. It is only "a peculiarly authoritative association within it." The state is determinate, a closed organization. Community may have definite historical shape and substance, it may have resting points on its way to its ultimate destiny, but it cannot have permanent boundaries.

While the state may give to a community a certain style or flavor, a certain structure to work with, the state is finally subordinate to community. Within itself the state cannot absolutize allegiance. Thus "The individual should not be summed up in his citizenship, otherwise the claim of citizenship will itself become a tyranny and its essential moral value be lost."[8]

THREE VALUE CLUSTERS IN AMERICAN LIFE

How, then, do "we sum ourselves up," if not in our citizenship? The answer, I think, is that each community employs its moral resources to define itself, and especially to say what it means by the "we relation." Not everyone says "we" alike, or means the same thing by it. What distinguishes one community from another is that each has its own "prior something," drawn from moral substance, that shapes its way of saying "we."

The loss of community in America is the loss of this "prior something," this way of saying "we," and of defining community. If we really want to understand the "death throes," we have to ask about these missing meanings or values, what they were like, how they held people together once, if not now.

I think there have been three important "value clusters" shaping community in American history. Each one adds up to an image, morally cast, of who "we" are. Sometimes one of these images would predominate over the other two. At another time, another image would come forward. There are certainly other options, other ways of arranging the moral strands, other ethics clusters, but I would contend that these three are central to the American experience:

1. The Puritan ethic of righteousness or obedience, in which the "prior value" is a *right will* as shaped by the electing grace of God.

2. The Revolutionary ethic of justice or dissent, in which the "prior value" is the *rights of man* philosophy with its affirmations of equality, dignity, and progress.

3. The Personal Encounter ethic of the voluntary

group and the commune, in which the "prior value" is the saving power of *intimate personal relationships* in the service of some vision.

But now I have used the word "ethic" (no "s") three times. Perhaps I had better say more plainly just what I mean by it. An ethic is a time-binding cluster of values that shapes, or partially shapes, the identity of a community. It has a reality on the order of true myths, which are discussed in the next chapter.

It is a mistake to write about an "ethic" without remembering the lives and deeds of those persons whose acts go toward expressing it; yet an ethic—such as the Puritan ethic of righteousness, or the Revolutionary ethic of justice, or the communards' ethic of encounter—takes on a supra-personal life, and has momentum, influence, and character far beyond the sum of the acts of the personal parties to it. That is why, in the discussions that follow, I have now and then "personified" the language I have used in speaking of these clusters. We often have trouble "seeing" the living reality of the three American clusters I have described because each of them has now become partly frozen, objectified, reified—in other words, seems to be dead or dying.[9]

Yet, in our history, each ethic, each of these value clusters, has made its mark on the American experience. Each has given rise to a succession of movements. Each has had its own special forms of community. Each has had its own distortions, abuses, and travesties.

The Puritan or righteousness ethic, stressing in its ideal pure form the electing grace of God, gave rise in the long run to the "Protestant work ethic," which in modified form became the leading value cluster in America. It is partly because this primary and influential value cluster has today become hardened, and in some ways harmful, that we are experiencing our time of troubles for community in America.

The Revolutionary ethic, stressing (at times one-sidedly) equality, dissent, reform, the crucial character of justice, is expressed not only in the views of a Thomas Jefferson or Tom Paine, but in the abolitionist movement, the later nineteenth-century Social Gospel, and such twentieth century phenomena as the early labor movement, the civil rights movement, and the civil liberties movement.

The Personal Encounter ethic is illustrated by such religious groups as the Quakers, with their stress on honesty, their distrust of formality and ritual in religious circles; by various nineteenth century communal experiments in America; and by such phenomena of our own day as the "New Morality" ("situation ethics"), the "Flower Children," the peace forces, Esalen-type groups, and contemporary experiments in communal living—each with its strengths and weaknesses.

Let us leave for later an examination of the ways in which each of these clusters has become diluted and distorted. First let's use our moral imagination and try to grasp the pure form or essence of each. Taken together they stand for what might be lost as bases of community in America.

Image I: An Overflowing Fountain

There is something about the Puritan experience that we can grasp by noting what happens in the life of a fictional character of our own day—S. Levin, the anti-hero of Bernard Malamud's novel, *A New Life*.[10]

S. Levin is a *schlemiel*, the poor guy who amounts to nothing, has luck go against him, and blunders into one failure after another. As the novel begins, Levin, a former alcoholic and young New York school teacher, has landed a college teaching job on the West Coast. Maybe he can make "a new life" out of it.

No such luck. Things keep going wrong. Levin looks

for a girl friend, and seems to have made it with a bar-maid, Laverne. They decide to go out into the country to make love. Laverne knows of a barn they can use. "My first barn," thought Levin to himself, contemplating how his life had changed in a month's time. "In front of cows," he thought. "Now I belong to the ages."

But the love-making was not to be. Someone sneaked into the barn, snatched their empty clothes and ran off. Distracted, they sneak back into town. Laverne breaks off with him.(The thief turned out to be Levin's jealous Syrian roommate.)

Then Nadalee, one of Levin's students, begins to flirt with him. Levin buys a car, with Nadalee in mind. He fails his drivers' license test, finally passes. Nadalee invites him to visit her at her aunt's deserted motel. Levin sets out, soon has car trouble. He gets it repaired, starts out again. He is soon stuck in a ditch, then he gets lost.

Worse things happen. Levin gets involved with Pauline, wife of his colleague, Gerald. Gerald finds out, forces Levin to resign. Meanwhile, Levin realizes that he doesn't love Pauline.

So what does he do? He *marries* her. And at this point, *S. Levin becomes a man.* For the first time in his life he holds his own as a human being.

What makes Levin is his discovery, at this late point, of the constitutive value of an act of will.

By the standards we usually use in measuring men, Levin was a failure. His life added up to little more than zero. But as Levin has his climactic encounter with Gerald, we see a different kind of "value" illustrated.

Gerald sarcastically describes what a bad deal Levin is getting in Pauline. "There are times when . . . she can't get organized enough to clean the toilet and I have to do it after a full day's work."

Gerald goes on to make clear he's going to blackball Levin, forcing him out of college teaching.

Knowing all this, Levin agrees to Gerald's terms.

"You're batty," said Gerald. "You're cutting your throat." Why would Levin do it? "An older woman than yourself and not dependable, plus two adopted kids, no choice of yours, no job or promise of one, and other assorted headaches. Why take that load on yourself?"

Levin's answer:

"Because I can, you son of a bitch."

Levin became a man because of the quality of his will, not because of his career (it was wrecked) or any set of lifelong accomplishments (there were none). Going against his inclinations, going against any rational calculation of what would be in his own best interest, Levin obligated himself to this woman as a thing that was *good in itself.*

There are vast differences between Levin and the Puritans, of course. The Puritans stressed that the very possibility of having a good will came from God. But the response was much the same: a cleaving to the will of God in one's own will was a good thing in itself.

Jonathan Edwards, who had perhaps the finest mind among all the Puritan divines of America, likened the love of God and its effects on the will to an overflowing fountain:

If man's affection to God is founded first on His profitableness to them, their affection begins at the wrong end; they regard God only . . . where it touches them and reaches their interest, and have no respect to that infinite glory of God's nature which is the original good, and the true fountain of all good, the first fountain of all loveliness of every kind. . . .[11]

What makes a man is the quality of his will, not his achievements, his attainments, the amount of money in his pocket, or what his neighbors think of him. Here the outlines of a community can be inferred. It is the right will, and those acts that flow from it, that bind men together.

There is a direct move, in this value cluster, from the right will to the structures of community. Men of right will express themselves in their acts and in their laws. "True grace is not an inactive thing," says Edwards. "There is nothing in heaven or earth of a more active nature; for it is life itself, and the most active kind of life, . . . *Godliness in the heart has as direct a relation to practice, as a fountain has to a stream, . . .*"[12]

The power of true godliness, then, lies "in its being effectual in practice." It will express itself not in private acts, either, for we are talking about a "temper of benevolence to being in general."[13] Because the right will aims at the well-being of the community, its ethic has a political character expressed in fondness for the rule of law and for political stability.[14]

This, then, is the righteousness ethic. It could also be called the right-will ethic, the good-will ethic, the duty ethic, or even the ethic of law and order. Community based upon this ethic flows, as a stream from a fountain, out of the intrinsic value of our commitments. We care for others out of a right will—out of a God-renewed heart, as the Puritans had it—and we care, not because there's anything in return guaranteed by that, but rather because binding oneself to the others and to the common good is, *in itself,* a worthwhile act, and its own reward. One looks to political stability and to the institutions of law to express righteousness in practice. It is an active public ethic in that the man of right will is citizen, engaged in his work, and amenable to the governmental process.[15]

The right will does not lay stress on attainment. "A true saint," Edwards says, "when in the enjoyment of true discoveries of the sweet glory of God and Christ, has his mind too much captivated and engaged by what he views without himself, to stand at that time to view himself, and his own attainments." Furthermore, "no external manifestations and outward appearances whatsoever, that are visible to the world, are infallible evidences of grace."[16]

That is Puritanism in its undistorted essence. But in our history, the righteousness ethic kept evolving. Its adherents forgot Edwards and focused upon secondary matters. God's grace was soon taken as a gift for which signs of its presence were to be eagerly sought. By and by these signs came to be more important than the gift itself. From there it was but a step to the easy acceptance in American morality of work and affluence as status signs of God's grace. This was a coverup, in effect, of the original central value: the significance of a right will in making men, and in establishing community. Finally, the notion of convincing God of anything (itself a drastic debasement of the original ethic) was dropped. Today only the secondary features, deprived usually of any relationship to the divine, remain in the "Protestant work ethic," which itself has all too often degenerated, as we shall see (Chapter IV), into a shabby display of legalism, obsession with property rights, undue individualism, superpatriotism, and frequent insensitivity to the proper concerns of the other two ethics clusters —justice and mutuality.

Image II: A Torch Passed On

In Sacramento, Calif., Robert H. Simpson celebrated his ninety-third birthday by going to the state capitol building and getting arrested—for the two hundred thirty-fourth time.

"Complaining is the first of your rights and you should preserve it," he said later. "When you can't complain, you're lost . . . Give me a scrap and I'll be happy forever."

Simpson, it appears, had been making a full-time av-
ocation of the citizen's right to protest against his government, indeed to the point of violating a California
law placing certain restrictions on demonstrating.

He was arrested so often that the state police developed a ritual. They would take him to jail each time,
but always release him and drop the complaint. "It's like
taking the cat out at night," one capitol policeman
commented.

Simpson stands in a long line of Americans and represents, in his way, one approach to the subject of moral
values in America.

Samuel Eliot Morison recounts an interview that took
place in 1842, between a judge and a ninety-one-year-
old veteran of the American Revolutionary Army.

"What made the farmers fight in 1775?" the judge
asked the old man. Was it the intolerable oppressions of
the British?

"Oppressions?" replied the veteran. "I didn't feel
them."

But wasn't the Stamp Act an oppression?

The old farmer answered that he had never seen even
one of the stamps, and he certainly hadn't paid out any
money for them.

Perhaps, then, went on the questioner, it was the tax
on tea.

"I never drank a drop of the stuff; the boys threw it
all overboard."

Then maybe the farmers had been reading Sidney,
Locke, or Harrington about the rights of man and the
ideals of liberty?

The old man allowed that he had never heard of
these men, and said that he and his fellows read little
more than the Bible, Watts' Psalms, and the Almanac.

What on earth was the matter, then? Why did they
fight?

"Young man, what we meant in going for those red-coats was this: we always had governed ourselves, and we always meant to. They didn't mean we should."[17]

For the Puritan mind, willing obedience to God and to law was the primary foundation of community. Justice, according to Jonathan Edwards, had only a "secondary and inferior kind of beauty." But with the Americans of the Revolutionary generation, the rights of man become primary. The leaders of 1776 found community in a shared sense of justice, of outrage at injustice (especially despotism), and an affirmation of dissent and countervailing action, even extending to questioning the law. Yet justice-seeking dissent rarely has erupted into outright rebellion or anarchy in America. Our founding revolution was a moderate one, as political revolutions go. Exemplars of the justice-dissent ethic in America usually call militantly for partial reforms extending into the future, not for complete overturn to bring in the new day forthwith.

All in all, we see here significant differences from the righteousness-duty ethic. The classic Puritan righteousness consisted of acts done of right will (love of God, benevolence to being, duty toward God, law, and neighbor, taken as ends), acts valuable in themselves, whatever the consequences. But for the advocate of the rights of man, the point of focus is not in the intent alone, the disposition, the motivation; it shifts rather to the goal of the intended act, out there beyond our wills—the human subject, his betterment, and his future.

Righteousness was, and is, a standard by which men are valued for the quality or sanctity of their wills. The Puritan commonwealth was of, by, and for the saints —those whose wills are right. A primary concern for justice, on the other hand, prompts us to value men as men, whether they are saints or not. It moves us much more quickly to the affirmation of the equality of all men, and to the importance of the historical future as the place appointed for the unfolding of the possibilities of community. What is intrinsically good for justice-seekers then, is not the already-achieved rightness of the will, but the forward-running hope of equality.

There are thus two motifs of importance for the making of community in the justice ethic.

First, the justice-seeker insists upon respect for the human person as such. The saintliness, lovableness, or talents of that person are beside the point. Community is built on respect for the other, and reciprocally upon levying his respect for me. This is no self-sacrificing stance: I am just as much entitled to your respect as you are to mine. Such respect does not have to be based on love or "benevolence to being." Hence communities arising out of the justice ethic provide for dissent, creative disruption, and reform in the interest of compelling respect.

On March 4, 1801, in his first inaugural address, President Thomas Jefferson asked the question of himself and of the people: What are the essential principles of our government?

The first, he said, was "Equal and exact justice to all men, of whatever state or persuasion, religious or political." He goes on to speak of "a jealous care of the right of election by the people," majority rule, and protection of minority rights, including freedom of religion, press, and person.[18]

Jefferson's statement amounts to a challenge of the classic righteousness ethic. He had long ago pushed, in fact, for the dismantling of some of the machinery that followers of the Puritans used to strengthen their own plan for community. In his earlier *Notes on Virginia* (1782) Jefferson almost casually recounts how the subject-matter taught at William and Mary was reorganized after the Revolution. Until then, as we could put it, the learning process in America had served to implement the righteousness ethic, having stressed the nurture of the soul by required theological study and the pursuit of Greek and Latin. After the Revolution, Jefferson reports, the college board of visitors excluded both its chairs of divinity, as well as the chair for the classical languages, and substituted others.[19] Men were now taken to be able to judge for themselves without theological massage of the mind and will. (A few years later, Tom Paine would put it boldly in *The Age of Reason:* "All national institutions of churches, whether Jewish, Christian, or Turkish, appear to me no other than human inventions, set up to terrify and enslave mankind, and monopolize power and profit."[20])

That cherished institution of the righteousness ethic, private property, was also to come under attack. In 1785 Jefferson, while living in France, had occasion to visit the court at Fontainebleau. On a long walk, he overtook a poor woman, and struck up a conversation.

The woman told Jefferson of having worked as a day laborer from the age of eight at pittance wages, and added that she often went without bread. Since she had given Jefferson advice on how to get to the nearby hills, he considered it fair to proffer a large tip. "She burst into tears of gratitude . . . She had probably never before received so great an aid."

Jefferson's reaction well illustrates one of the deepest moral values of the justice-dissent ethic. This episode in Fontainebleau, he tells us, "led me into a train of reflections on that unequal division of property which occasions . . . numberless instances of wretchedness."

He goes on to say that legislators ought to begin to find ways for more widely distributing property. Startlingly, he proposes, as one means of "silently lessening the inequality of property," to exempt the poor from taxes, "and to tax the higher portions or property in geometrical progression as they rise." He indignantly concludes that "the laws of property have been so far extended as to violate natural right. The earth is given as a common stock for man to labor and live on."[21]

Jefferson (as Lincoln would) speaks of the right of revolution. In a famous letter written from Paris in 1787, he even proclaims, "God forbid we should ever be twenty years without such a rebellion" as the American Revolution. What country can preserve its liberties, he asks, "if its rulers are not warned from time to time, that this people preserve the spirit of resistance?"[22]

More typically, however, the protagonists of the justice ethic call for dissent of a moderate, time-binding character, such as the call of Jefferson himself in his inaugural address of 1801. Protests are in order, he says, against political abuses; but the abuses should be attacked with "mild and safe" correctives, and promptly, lest they be "lopped by the sword of the revolution where peaceable remedies are unprovided."[23]

Thus for the justice ethic the first intrinsic value and the basis of community is in the natural birthright of a human being. Jefferson was a man of his times and shared the usual prejudices about the black man's talents, intelligence, and capability. Nevertheless, he insists, "whatever be their degree of talent it is no measure of their rights. Because Sir Isaac Newton was superior to others in understanding, he was not therefore lord of the person or property of others."[24]

Here, then, is the first motif of community in the justice ethic: respect for man as man, "equal and exact justice to all." The second motif flows out of the first: a strong orientation toward the future. Present communities are only partly real, because they have not yet experienced the full meaning of equality. The imperative, then, is: push on toward the future. Community is won by "passing the torch along" from one generation to the next. Justice cannot be satisfied by present arrangements. Human rights, and thus community, at every present moment are lessened by abuse from tyrants and the selfish—a problem not just for Europe but for our side of the Atlantic too, according to Jefferson.[25] The challenge is to seek to do better—through dissent, prophecy, reform, reconstruction.

There are worse things than overriding the law, according to Jefferson:

... A strict observance of the written laws is doubtless *one* of the high duties of a good citizen, but it is not *the highest*. The laws of necessity, of self-preservation, of saving our country when in danger, are of higher obligation. To lose our country by a scrupulous adherence to written law, would be to lose the law itself, with life, liberty, property and all those who are enjoying them with us; thus absurdly sacrificing the end to the means.[26]

We should not be surprised to find many of these themes echoed in Abraham Lincoln's thought, for Lincoln declared: "The principles of Jefferson are the definitions and axioms of a free society."[27]

The revolutionary fathers, Lincoln said, "meant to set up a standard maxim" for our liberties. It would be well known to all—revered, looked to, worked for. Though it would never be "perfectly attained," it would still be "constantly approximated." Indeed, he declares, the assertion that "all men are created equal" was in itself of little practical value in gaining independence from Great Britain. "And it was placed in the Declaration, not for that, but for future use."[28]

At this point we have to remark on a flaw in the justice ethic. Its strength conceals a weakness that by the twentieth century would haunt us. The seeker of justice wishes to look to the future, and is prepared to question

present laws and existing political stability. The problem
comes from the presumption that reform will take time.
There will always be those who say: "We can't wait,
change must come now." Others will always argue that
laws once disregarded threaten community by undermining all respect for law. Where does one draw the
line?

There is, in short, a maddening relativism necessarily
present in the justice ethic. It is there in the thought of
both Jefferson and Lincoln. Utility, Jefferson declares
in one of his most reflective letters on the subject, is "the
standard and test of virtue." But utility is a relative
thing: "Men living in different countries, under different circumstances, different habits and regimens, may
have different utilities; the same act, therefore, may be
useful, and consequently virtuous in one country which
is injurious and vicious in another differently
circumstanced."[29]

Lincoln's thought shows another form of the same
problem. Hope in the future may be shaded in either
direction—toward more rapid change, in order to rescue equality and dignity; or toward more drawn out
change in order to preserve stability. The more insistent
abolitionists found Lincoln too content with the second
of these approaches. And we do sense, at points, some
foot-dragging. In his debates with Stephen A. Douglas,
Lincoln continually stressed that the framers of the
Constitution "intended and expected the ultimate extinction" of slavery—that is, not the extinction of it right
away. He was prepared to join the opponents of slavery
in an effort to "resist the farther spread of it," confident
that "the public mind shall rest with the belief that it is in
course of ultimate extinction."[30]

The struggle for justice has depended all along in
American history on compromise, reform by legisla-
tion, forward steps as and where possible. Indeed, the

justice ethic is like the righteousness ethic in that its exemplars commonly seek political solutions. More than once, in an extreme situation, the justice-seeker has settled for order now, change later. "Much as I hate slavery," Lincoln said, "I would consent to the extension of it rather than see the Union dissolved, just as I would consent to any GREAT evil, to avoid a GREATER one."[31]

Yet the compromising of ideals has been accepted, within the tradition of the American justice ethic, as a price worth paying. Slavery was abolished, the Union preserved, and the torch passed on. In the twentieth century perhaps the best moments for the justice ethic came with the civil rights movement of the 1960's—a movement that lately seems to have undergone its own malaise of community. The non-violent protests led by Martin Luther King, Jr., were effective calls for new steps toward dignity, and they were fully in the tradition operating through public, forceful action aimed at changing laws and eliciting respect. Even the more electric militance displayed by the Black Muslims was within the tradition. Here is Malcolm X on the subject:

> I'm not for wanton violence, I'm for justice. . . . I *am* for violence if non-violence means we continue postponing a solution to the American black man's problems—just to *avoid* violence . . . If it must take violence to get the black man his rights in this country, I'm *for* violence exactly as you know the Irish, the Poles, or Jews would be if they were flagrantly discriminated against. . . . The Negro's so-called "revolt" is merely an asking to be *accepted* into the existing system![32]

From Jefferson to Malcolm X, the spirit of the justice-dissent ethic is to found community upon the possibilities natively present in man as man—with no test made of his sainthood. The justice-seeker, then and now, has been willing to test the law and (up to a point)

to risk political stability. Recent permutations of this
spirit, have placed greater stress on the rights of the
underprivileged masses, than upon the status of the individual. Alongside the ideal of work championed by
the Puritans and their successors, this justice-seeking
company of Americans has raised the watchword of reform. Instead of affluence as a sign of righteousness,
redistribution of property becomes a goal. Prophetic
criticism, is a virtue prized above obedience. And, on
the negative side, there is an ambiguous relativism in
the justice ethic that matches the equally dangerous
tendency toward repression of the righteousness ethic.

Men and women dedicated first of all to justice have
furthered profound advances in the quality and scope
of community in America. To see this, we need only
turn to a series of events in our past—abolitionist
movements, the Social Gospel, civil disobedience
movements, the civil rights movement of recent times.
Even so, the story is not a totally happy one. Although
the justice-dissent ethic represents the moderately revolutionary spirit of our founding fathers, it has normally been a secondary force in American life, much
less influential than the righteousness ethic. It has never
had a a fair chance to serve as the basis for widespread
community in this country. And that is one reason many
Americans have rejected both of the politically oriented
ethics clusters and have warmed themselves at a third
fire, another basis for community

Image III: Common Cup, Common Cause

In the old adventure comic strips like *Terry and the
Pirates,* a dramatic story line is pursued. National
enemies are tracked down, or criminals are chased, or
shady characters are exposed by the derring-do of one
or more heroes and heroines. But in the new comics
that have replaced some of the older strips there is

neither the high drama of the pursuit, nor the slapstick or belly laugh of such entries as *Mutt and Jeff*. Instead, we are offered mordant comment on issues of the day.

Prehistoric characters talk about the high price of food. Animals show up who look suspiciously like a former Vice President. Kids chatter about the energy crisis. Comics have gone political. Some cartoonists —Jules Feiffer is one of them—have in effect moved from the comics page to the editorial page. Maybe they belong there.[33]

There is still another trend in the new comics illustrated by *Doonesbury*, a "hip" strip created by Garry Trudeau. *Doonesbury* seems to have a split personality. There are, to be sure, plenty of political days—biting take-offs on the foibles of the White House, for example. But other days *Doonesbury* goes off in a different direction. As I sit at my breakfast table and read *Doonesbury* in the Houston *Post* (on the days the editors have not censored it) I get the feel of a new kind of comment about American community.

For often, in these certain *Doonesbury* strips, as in some other new comics, the "action" is neither comic nor political—nor is it action. Often the point seems to depend on having no action at all. There is generally a laugh, but it is a painful one, a rueful laugh produced at the spectacle of people sitting around trying to relate to each other, and not always succeeding.

One *Doonesbury* strip shows a college football team in its huddle. (This huddle is a frequent fixture.) There is no football playing going on. There is no planning of strategy. The huddle is really an encounter group or commune. And the subject matter of the players' talk isn't football; it's human relationships. The stern captain (does he have darker lines around his eyes than the other players?) singles out and rakes over Zonker, a freaky loser on the team. Zonker wears a beard, and you can see long hair creeping out from underneath his helmet. Zonker's helmet isn't regulation. Other team members have one star on each side of their helmets. Zonker's is covered with stars.

The captain rails at him. "Zonker, ever since you joined the team, you've been a pain, a nuisance, and a general trouble maker!" Zonker stands silently. He breaks and begins to cry. Finally his tears turn to bawling. The other members of the team chide the captain: "Now look what you've done, you bully." And comfort Zonker: "Poor guy!" "He didn't mean it, Zonker." Zonker continues to sob and sniff. End of strip.

On another occasion, the captain's busty, casually coiffed girl friend runs out to the huddle, just before the game begins, and lays a good-luck kiss on the captain, who smiles euphorically at that. Zonker, thinking to show his good spirit also, rises from the huddle, and plants his own good-luck kiss. The captain explodes with rage, while Zonker, back down in the huddle, mutters to himself about the captain's chapped lips. End of strip.

All of this is comic only in a bittersweet sense. If the comics of past years and generations celebrated, in their own ways, the national myths and dilemmas, it is possible to suppose that the new types, like *Doonesbury, Peanuts,* and *Beetle Bailey* also convey something about the state of mind in America. Such comics are commentaries on the demise of community in America. And they point to a *third way out* that has been sought by people in America for solving the problem of community.

This third way, which stands in contrast to both the righteousness ethic and to the justice ethic, we may call the ethic of personal encounter. For its devotees the highest good is found in warm, intense person-to-person relationships, in intimate common life. They want a style of community more directly akin to the intimacy we discovered earlier with the Packer family. Again, as with the other two clusters, the associated motifs are greatly varied, and we could have called it something else with equal plausibility: the voluntary group ethic, the dialogue syndrome, the communitarian impulse, and so forth.

Community based upon this third combination of values has sprung into fragile new life in our times —with new nature communes, apostles of "The New Morality," peace movements, "Flower Children," human potentials groups, and the like. As different as the groups may be among themselves, all have in common a quest for meaningful relationships. They are only the latest in a long line of attempts at an alternative way toward community in America. The encounter ethic, however, is doubtless even more a junior partner than the justice ethic in the ongoing life of the country: up to and including our own times, the communitarian groups have tended to spring up on the fringes of society, or to withdraw from the clamor of public life, and to suffer a high mortality rate.

One historic root of the personal-encounter ethic lies in the radical groups that come out of the Reformation. Their leaders talk about living holy lives together, whereas leaders of the "mainline" Reformation, beginning with Luther and Calvin, focus upon right belief. God's grace works when we lay hold in faith, argue the main-liners. God's grace shows itself directly in renewed living, respond the radicals. Because the world at large is evil and not disposed toward holy life, the radicals as a rule set themselves apart in small congregations, gathered together in isolation. By contrast the faith of Lutherans, Calvinists, Anglicans, as with the American Puritans, led to a public style of obedience.

"In this community," writes Ulrich Stadler, leader of a

sixteenth-century Bohemian group of Anabaptists, "everything must proceed equally, all things . . . one and communal." He urged his brethren to "live with one another . . . peaceable, united, lovingly, amicably, . . . altogether as one body and members toward one another." True friends, he said, "have all things in common; indeed, they are called two bodies with but one soul."[34] Groups such as the Amish, Hutterites, and Mennonites, settling in America from the seventeenth century on, planted this heritage. To this day, many of them have preserved their traditional communities, and "in a manner so withdrawn," Sidney Ahlstrom comments, "that until fairly recently they have existed on the American scene more as a picturesque souvenir . . . than as an influence on the nation's religious life."[35]

The most notable exemplars of the encounter ethic in America flourished in the nineteenth century. Some groups were religious, some secular. Usually perfectionist, all were critical of the conventional institutions of American society. They withdrew from the public structures of life and established themselves in closely knit communal societies. Most of them did not last long, but some are well remembered. The Amana Society is commemmorated today in the name of a freezer. The Oneida perfectionists left their name behind in a famous make of silverware. New England literary figures spread the fame of Brook Farm. There were also the Icarians, the Aurora and Bethel communes, the Separatists of Zoar, and many others.

These groups were certainly not all alike. Their interests and policies varied hugely. At Oneida the perfectionists practiced a system of plural marriage. The Shakers, on the other hand, practiced celibacy, also out of a spirit of perfectionism. Sometimes outright legalism was employed to serve the ends of encounter—which need not be a contradiction at all. As one of my Rice students living in a small commune explained: "We have to have rules if we're going to love each other well. No more than three persons in group sex. No homosexuality." For some of the nineteenth-century groups, the rules extended to: no sex, period. But that led, in their view, to even more intense relationships on other bases.

Despite their vast differences, these groups did share some crucial values for building community.

One of the overriding values emphasized the *voluntary* character of community. Advocates of the righteousness ethic see the state, with its requirements of obedience to law, compulsory schools, and so forth, as the proper context for protecting the interest of community. Reformists of the justice-dissent ethic value the state and compulsory procedures, too, not so much as guardians of the status quo as enablers of future respect and dignity. The view we are now describing differs from both, holding that the most important bond of community is free relationship among consenting associates. There is often, indeed, a kind of alienation from the dominant institutions and associations of society—from the big churches as well as from the state.

The career of John Humphrey Noyes, founder of the Oneida community, is illustrative. Born in Vermont in 1811, Noyes was impressed, as a college student, by the revival fervor of the times, and shifted from law to theology. He had all the makings of another orthodox revivalist, serving the establishment. His father had been a Congressman. His mother was the aunt of Rutherford B. Hayes, our nineteenth president. But Noyes became "one of the most extreme revolutionaries that Western Civilization has produced"[36]—not in a political sense, but in moral and cultural spheres.

Noyes was a religious perfectionist, a socialist, and a radical critic of conventional sex morality. Among his theological teachings were such shockers as this: "God is dual," i.e., both male and female at once. He taught perfectionism out of his view that "The Bible predicts the coming of the Kindgom of Heaven on earth." His views on sex were just as unacceptable to American society as was his theology. If the Kingdom of Heaven is truly at hand, then it is clear that "the institution of marriage, which assigns the exclusive possesson of one woman to one man, does not exist." Christ's new commandment is that we love one another all around, and not just "by pairs." A better arrangement is "a Community home in which each is married to all, and where love is honored and cultivated."[37]

Thus evolved the notion of "complex marriage." Each adult was married to all of the others. Special pairing off between a husband and wife was forbidden as possessiveness, which is just as wrong "when it relates to persons, as when it relates to money or any other property."

These teachings took concrete form first at Putney, Vermont, then later at Oneida, New York, where Noyes re-established his commune. Just after the Civil War Noyes reported that the community had 202 members. They lived in a large brick dwelling called the "Community Home." The home symbolized the vision. "The organic principle of Communism in industry and domestic life," Noyes said, "is seen in the common roof, the common table, and the daily meetings of all the members."

Among the industries of the commune were the manufacture of steel traps (more than a quarter million in 1868), preserving fruits, silk-making, the casting of iron, and eventually silver-plated flatware. There was a sawmill, a dairy, and farmlands that produced potatoes, strawberries, apples, and grapes. The community had its own shoemakers, tailors, and dentists."[38]

With time the religious fervor faded, and with it

Noyes' vision of the Kingdom on earth. The community moved toward a secular outlook. Externally, the situation was even worse. The Oneida Community "crashed head on into the most sacred institution in Victorian America: the monogamous family."[39] The pressure was more than the community could stand. It became a business corporation, its struggle against the establishment abandoned.

Noyes taught one thing, other communes something else. But his career, and the experience at Oneida, does show us one common feature of these groups. All believed that community was constituted by men and women free to renounce conventional society and to join in a new voluntary undertaking. Franklin Littell suggests that a study of the history of the communes and sectarian religious groups gives us "some sense of the extent to which voluntary community of a most thoroughgoing kind helped to articulate and to shape the American dream."[40]

And so the locus of community shifts; it is no longer based in a righteous will devoted to public order. It is not conceived as a future prospect for the rights of man. In the encounter ethic, community stems from the *realized quality of personal human relationships*. Such quality can come only in a freely joined-in rather than coerced or mandated association.

A contemporary call to return to the voluntary community comes from Theodore Roszak, in *Where the Wasteland Ends*. Dismayed by the blindness of science to deeper meanings, appalled by the ravages of urbanism and technocracy, frustrated by the wrong-headedness of politics, Roszak seeks a countervailing "visionary commonwealth." Many today are awakening to "transcendent longings," he says, and are seeking to band together "to find like-minded others, to become this special group unto itself: the commune, the one place in all the fierce, foolish world where men and women may call their souls their own." Those of this persuasion "simply have better things to do with themselves than play power politics." They seek spiritual growth, and the peace and personal intimacy that permits it."And that means the life of small, congenial groups."[41]

We are reminded again of Alfred Schutz and the "we-relation." While community may indeed be furthered by the status of my will on yours, and by future progress in human rights, there is a more central affirmation to be made. And this is the claim that community is built up out of the mutuality between us, which introduces a new reality greater than the wills, or the hopes, of either of us taken separately.

Besides voluntarism, there is a second important common value in the encounter ethic. It has to do with the institution of property. Littell thinks the property issue, in fact, is the main theme that unites the communal movements of the nineteenth century:

Although the Shakers and Oneida gave major attention to sexual ethics, and several of the communities had special doctrines of divine inspiration or types of charismatic leadership, the issue which relates them uniquely is the attitude to property. The basic claim to property is *use* rather than possession of title. Material things exist for the common good, *in stewardship,* rather than for individual or private satisfaction.[42]

Let us carefully note that this attitude to property is not limited to the communes. It has proved to be one of the most appealing attributes of the encounter ethic, having captured the spirit of many of the young in our society today who do not live in communes. I made this discovery by accident. I was fascinated to observe, over a period of eighteen months to two years, how this indifference-to-property trait took hold in the mind of my teen-age daughter, Lucy.

During her senior year of high school I began to notice the change. In her early teens she voiced many of the same uncritical attitudes as numerous other middle-class offspring: "When I get married I might as well look around for some guy who has money, or is going to be able to make a pile."

Then, within the year, a tide of second thoughts. She attended a national convention of her high school sorority, came home puzzled and disappointed by the racism of some of the sisters from Alabama and Mississippi. Shortly afterward she resigned from the sorority, also resigned as a cheerleader, dropped her demands that I buy her a car for college, settled for a bicycle instead.

One night during her freshman spring semester at the University of Houston, we had her friend Beth, from Sweet Briar College, as a houseguest. We were talking at dinner that evening about whether college really helped anyone nowadays to become happy and fulfilled. Lucy and Beth voiced the current chic disillusionment, and I had to agree.

"Most colleges don't really teach you how to think for yourself." I went from there into my standard rationale for staying in college, anyway—showing how much I am a prisoner of the watered down righteousness ethic: "In any case, a college education will program you so that you can make more money."

"Who cares about making more money?" they shot back. Neither Lucy nor Beth has, at this writing, joined a commune. But the shift in values I witnessed in them over these months does illustrate that there is a live alternative view of community and of property afloat. If it is most intensively expressed in the life of the commune, its spirit is nonetheless more widely available.

An analysis of the contemporary kibbutz movement in Israel, by Douglas Sturm, maintains that it was not only the arduous labor of the members that explains its flowering; it is also, and more deeply, a question of living out the "spirit of Israel."

Very few of the kibbutz members are specifically religious. But that should not mislead us, says Sturm, who argues that "the ground of the kibbutzim is the religious spirit of Israel." Withal, there is a strong "utopian vision" drawn out of the ideals, and ultimately out of the religious heritage, of the members. This utopian thrust is in constant tension with the more pragmatic interests of the kibbutzim, but both sides of the tension are necessary.

> The fundamental vision of the kibbutz movement is in effect of a new heaven and a new earth, or more modestly, of a new society and a new man. This is the vision that arises out of the influences from whose combination the movement emerged—particularly Zionism and socialism. These "isms" are retained as part of the basic belief structure and mythology of the most dedicated kibbutzniks even while a significant number of younger members of the kibbutzim are more or less cynical about the ideology and more pragmatic. . . .[43]

Here is a clue to the notable failure rate of "dropout" movements. To generate lasting community, the alternative offered by encounter must have goals other than the satisfaction of getting in touch with one another, and of letting the world go by. It must have a cause to go after. It must be a movement not just of withdrawal-from, but also of gathering-for.

Our ideal exemplar of the encounter ethic, then, is embodied in a voluntary community where mutuality exists, where goods are shared, and which is "glued together" by a common cause, warmed at the fire of a vision. It must be more than a community of dissatisfaction with the mainline American style of life. It must present some alternative lifestyle, and that in the double form of a dream that can be pursued in the daily work and lives of the members.

LOOKING BEYOND THE LOSSES

We have described community as the "we-relation" in our lives, taken across time, manifested at personal, marketplace, and national levels, and generated by a definite value system. I have identified three ideal value clusters in the American experience that seem to me to have been at the bottom of the most significant expressions of community in this country up until now: the righteousness ethic, the justice ethic, and the encounter ethic.

In emphasizing the discreteness of these three value clusters, I may have underplayed the overlaps, alliances, and healthy tensions among them. The "reform" impulse in America, for example, I have identified with the justice ethic; but many of the communes of the nineteenth century were zealously devoted to reform. The encounter ethic I have described as taking shape in separated voluntary communities; but there are advocates of the encounter ethic who see human community as primarily universal, such as nineteenth-century romantics and transcendentalists.

There are certainly other ways of arranging the clusters, and other possible clusters. The South, some would say, had an approach to community all its own. So far, I have spoken very little of a "nature ethic" or an "ecology cluster" that some will argue to be as important for community as the three clusters I have chosen to employ. (But see Chapter VI.)

The three clusters I have identified do seem to me to have been at the heart of things in this country. They are ways of describing the "inner fires" that warm up the human prospect and make community possible. They are perspectives on our heritage, prisms for the benefit of our moral imagination. They are aids for reflection when we talk about what might now be lost.

Today, as we have seen, the very notion of community in America is seriously called into question. The principal reason, I believe, is that the ethical clusters which have always underwritten American community have in our day lost their inward meaning. But one of the most enigmatic sayings of the Christian Gospel suggests that awareness of loss may be the best way to get on the right path again: "Whoever seeks to gain his life will lose it, but whoever loses his life will preserve it" (Luke 17:33). Loss of community is, of course, a negative entry in the ledger of life; yet seeing that loss for what it is, or could be, may be a larger gain than we ever imagined. I will try, in the next chapter, to show why this is so.

III

Seeing America

WHAT'S IN a chance knock at the door? Enough, it turned out, to give me pause—and a clue. I was reading about the first lunar landing. My mind was 200,000 miles away, with Armstrong and Aldrin at Tranquillity Base. It was the Bellefontaine Apartments, for a change, that were unreal.

Then a knock brought me back. Not an ordinary knock, but a knock of the "Shave and a haircut—two bits" variety. That and more, as if a progressive jazz drummer had decided to play a theme and variations, and had done it with dancing knuckles on my front door.

One of my students, I thought. But the only student who ever used the "Shave and a Haircut" routine now lived in Denver. Besides, she never showed such flair for cadenza. I opened the door and there was a tall young black—a stranger.

"Man, I got all sortsa things to sell ya," he began, unfurling a strand of plastic display pictures. He talked on a minute, then I broke in.

"Can't think of a thing I need." (Here's the tough urban apartment-dweller, braced for the insensitive aggressor.)

"Then you very fortunate, man," he amiably replied. He folded up his display cards and disappeared into the night.

Out of that wispiest encounter with a stranger came a puzzling second thought. Somehow, in assembling the evidence about America's lack of community, I had missed a piece. That fancy knock didn't fit the pattern. Without the jazzdrummerlike knock, I'd no doubt have taken the man for a dangerous militant, and all my evidence about America's demise would have been confirmed. But not with it. Whatever the differences between him and me—race, age, his have-notness, my having-enoughness, his wish to sell, my determination not to buy—we had something in common.

What? First of all, the knock itself. A mutual appreciation for the percussive roll of "Shave and a Haircut." As long as there's a guy out there, otherwise alienated, who goes around giving out with such door knocks, things can't be all bad. A man has to have a reason for knocking like that.

One can have a reason without even knowing it. To find out what such reasons are, or might be, to find out what the unknown man at the door believed, or might have believed, not only about himself, but about me: that is the business of the moral imagination.

Fed up with America's racism, James Baldwin exiled himself to the other side of the Atlantic. By and by he realized that in, with, and under his discontents, he was still an American. Frantz Fanon, in his interpretation of the revolution in Algeria, talks about the gap that stands between Africa's black leaders and America's. The

American blacks, I thought he was saying, were in fundamental ways closer to me, whitey, their honky adversary, than they were to their own African brothers: "negritude therefore finds its first limitation in the phenomena which take account of the formation of the historical character of men . . . the problems which kept Richard Wright or Langston Hughes on the alert were fundamentally different from those which might confront Leopold Senghor or Jomo Kenyatta."[1]

So the knock, for me, was more than a chance incursion by an unauthorized salesman breaking the Bellefontaine's rules against soliciting. It was a symbolic question addressed to me—by a mythic messenger—about what it meant to be an American. It was a forceful reminder that whatever the national disarray, the bedrock reality of communication—which is, after all, the evocation of something-in-common—was still occurring. How to account for it, how to drag it out into the open was the question—out of me, out of my own inwards; out of ourselves; out of our crisis of community.

A NEW TRY AT READING WHAT'S THERE

One reason for not seeing something, of course, is that it's not there. Another reason for not seeing something is that we may be using the wrong instruments for looking. You can't find your way around Copenhagen with a map of Europe, though Copenhagen may appear on that map. You can't find out how much students know about "ethics," I have found, by giving them conventional tests requring rote memory work. Often when we're looking for something, we miss "seeing" it because of inappropriate images in our minds. Everything depends, on seeing a challenge appropriately. What are the appropriate ways of seeing the decline of community in America?

First, let us review two tried-and-true approaches. One of them has it that this decline represents a betrayal of our own history, and that the solution is to return to the past for refueling of those warming fires now going out. Let us call this approach, for brevity, the resort to history.

The second way, almost a trademark of the American mind, is to write off the past as unimportant, anyway, to reason that nothing up to here really matters, and to seek a brand-new community in the future. Let us call this approach, for brevity, the appeal to futurity.

1. The Resort to History

This collection of people in America certainly had community of a sort at one time, runs this scenario; what we need to do is recover the lost past. This attempt to recover the past picked up steam with the approach of America's bicentennial celebrations. But it has been a popular recourse for many years. Most of us have seen the phenomenon at work. We have been crushed in crowds at Gettysburg. We know people who have memorized the stops along the Natchez Trace Parkway almost in the way devout Catholics learn the stations of the cross. The Alamo vies with Greenfield Village in Dearborn as America's Times Square of the past.

But what are these hordes of tramping Americans really looking for? The guts and sinews of their heritage, the values that once gave men courage and community? Or are they searching for an escape, a simpler era, a supposedly happier day, an idealized past that never really existed? "In this access of nostalgia," *Newsweek* commented, "Americans seem to want to see and touch

anything old—the genuine old, if possible, but even the
hokey and plastic 'old' will do if nothing better is available." Thus Silver Dollar City, Mo., a nineteenth-century
village, packs them in even though it was invented from
scratch in 1963 by a designer of movie sets (its buildings
are only five-eighths true size.) The mixed character of
Americans' touring interests is shown in this list, from
the Commerce Department, of the seven most popular
"man-made wonders" in the country:

> Golden Gate Bridge, San Francisco
> Mt. Rushmore National Memorial
> Astrodome, Houston
> Statue of Liberty
> Hoover Dam
> Disney World, Florida
> Gateway Arch, St. Louis[2]

One of the deepest problems with the resort to the
past is that Americans do not, in general, display an unusual sense of history, as in many European communities. We are used to thinking our way out of crises
with the resources of space rather than those of time:
move across the bay; go west; pull up stakes; hit the
road.

This American indifference and even resistance to
history came to poignant focus among the anti-war
young a few years ago. Their refusal of the past is
dramatically illustrated by a character in Jean Anouilh's
play *Le Voyageur sans Bagages.* The central character,
Gaston, is a shell-shocked amnesiac, but something
more than a man who has simply lost his memory in the
war. When he discovers, on presentation of the evidence, who he really was, and how cruel and inhumane
he had been in his early life, he prefers to renounce it,
to deny that he is actually Jacques Renaud. He finds an
ingenious way to do so, and tells Valentine, the

sister-in-law who remains in love with him, why he is not coming back:

I am in the act of refusing my past and its personages —myself included. Perhaps you are my family, my loves, my true history. Yes, but . . . I refuse you.[3]

To do that, Valentine argues, would be foolish. It would make one a moral monster. "No one can refuse his past. No one can refuse himself." But Gaston persists. Destiny does not give everyone such a chance to wipe out the past and start fresh. "Not to take advantage of such an opportunity would be criminal. I refuse you."

From the point of view of the protesting students, America's past, especially its recent past, was one of such moral blindness—unjust wars, racism, corruption, lying, and spying—that it must be refused. And this generation, like Gaston, had an unusual chance, almost by way of a *deus ex machina,* to do so. This generation, at least for a while, could sit it out. For unlike earlier generations, it had few bills to pay.

For many of this generation, moreover, refusal of the past was not accompanied, in the older American style, by compensatory zeal about the future.

For some students of the recent past, American shallowness about history evolved into a view of America as a downright unsatisfying, meaningless, or even morally dubious patrimony. But for some there came, in time, the equivalent of that knock at my door that cynicism can't account for. A young North Dakotan wrote me from Toronto, where he was pursuing graduate studies. He had been away from the U.S. for five years and was reluctant to return. America wasn't worth it. And yet, he couldn't quite get the American experience out of his system, he couldn't quite accept the argument that it was somebody else's dirty past that we were talking about.

Maybe he still wanted, he said in his letter, to find some way decently "to admit to being an American." But how can we, he asked, even if we think well of the American heritage, possibly "recover a heritage virtually destroyed during the 60's?" Could the American tradition be reclaimed from its recent disappointing leaders? Could it be rescued from misuse as an instrument of aggression?

Part of the answer to these questions, and to our larger question of recovering community, does lie in the American past. Part of the way there does lie in the work of historians, and in the efforts of citizens to comprehend their own legacy. Part of the way there does lie, as I have suggested, in the challenge to recover those "warming fires" on which community was built—righteousness, justice, and mutuality. As we have seen, however, these three expressions of an American ethic have become hardened. If we are to recapture the light and warmth of those fires that burnt in the past, we must find a new setting for them—and that means a resolute examination of present and future.

2. The Appeal to Futurity

A second way of coping with crisis is ready to hand in the consciousness of Americans. And that is to seek America's destiny in the future, forgetting the past. We hear and see numerous versions of this alternative.

The most flamboyant is the approach of the futurologists. Their epigrams tell us the story of change, and they reel them off as matter-of-factly as disc jockeys giving the weather forecast:

"Those under the age of twenty-five are the first generation in human history to grow up in a contraceptive culture."

"A nerve network of copper wire and satellite reflectors encircle[s] our globe to reach not just the scientific community but every man."

". . . Cloning (producing a group of organisms, asexually, from a single common ancestor), will be with us within a decade or two. . . . The results [might] be a dozen or a hundred of your identical twins, your xeroxed body minus a few years."[4]

The futurologists are dead right, of course. The future is going to force just such drastic changes upon us. How do we deal with these shocks, how do we treat them morally, how do we recover community after crossing this Rubicon of the calendar, this time warp to 2001?

If our technology takes a quantum jump, says the futurologist, so must our values. Received moralities and ethical systems were for the turtle-like change scale of the past. If they seem to be in decline, that may be a good rather than a bad thing. Let them go, let the old fires burn out. That only saves us the trouble of extinguishing them anyway. There are new fuels ahead, new fires that will dance high, make the old ones pale by comparison.

For every zig of technology, we might say, the futurologist demands that we come up with a zag in ethics.

But are we not being treated here to a serious begging of the question? It is easy to grant the inevitability of change, of *drastic* change, and the corresponding need for appropriate values. But what are "new" values made of? Where do they come from?

Values are more like symbols, myths, and folklore than like transistors, skylabs, and computers. Values grow and die and answer to crises, and in new epochal crises, answering values arise. But no one produces them in a laboratory. No one thinks them up deliberately, any more than we think up our heritage. No one can fix them when they really begin to fail. What the late theologian Paul Tillich says about symbols applies pretty much to values, and to those ethical clusters that we have been metaphorically summing up as "warming fires":

> . . . A symbol opens up levels of reality which otherwise are closed for us . . . it opens up hidden depths of our own being. . . . But symbols cannot be produced intentionally. . . . They grow out of the individual or collective unconscious. . . . Symbols cannot be invented. . . . They grow when the situation is ripe for them, and they die when the situation changes.[5]

Symbols, we might add, grow out of themselves. And so do values and ethics clusters. Every live ethic, every functioning value system, is a kaleidoscopic reshaping amid crisis of the old, a combination of the old and the new. In America today, for example, old tribal values that sanctioned large families and procreation for the purpose of carrying on the name are being transformed. There is a new emphasis upon the freedom of women to choose some other life than child-bearing. And yet the "new" value summed up in the epithet "women's rights" is an adaptation in new circumstances of a primordial American value summed up in the epithet "rights of man." Successive twists of the kaleidoscope of history showed that this value yields, also, the rights of blacks, the rights of other non-WASPS, the rights of eighteen-year-olds, with more to come.

Another modality of seeking community in the future is to posit one's hopes on a forthcoming revolution. Like the futurologists, most revolutionaries seem to wish henceforth to build a world without drawing on the used-up hypostasis of America-as-it-was. I am more sympathetic with the revolutionaries than with the futurologists. America no doubt needs a revolution, although de Tocqueville made it rather clear in his *L'Ancien Régime et la Révolution* that such upheavals stand little chance of sloughing off the past: both the strengths and weaknesses of the new regime are often cultural inheritances from the old.

In any case, America, I suspect, will never have another revolution, if we mean by that a drastic political overturn. Although community, in the sense of common fidelity, may seem in demise just now, other structural bonds remain strong, the bonds of national business, of federal power, and of middle-class property holding, for examples. We need both a political and a moral revolution, to be sure, but we must hope for their benefits by other routes—one of which I mean to propose presently.

More commonplace, doubtless more representative of future orientation in America, is the success ethic of the business mind. The "old values" are talked of constantly—but they seem to lie nowhere but down the road in the future. And they may be secured only by forward motion—by growth, bettering sales quotas, throwing in with the team, and besting the competition. At its best, this is an honorable approach, for what it is intended to accomplish. At its worst it becomes something pathological.[6] In any case, however, what is garnered is scarcely a revival of community fires. A rising sales curve, however important in its place, is not the herald of an ample future, but in some ways is part of the problem.

The ideals that underwrite community are alloys of past values and future hopes, fused into something new by the present crisis. Thus when we attempt to find ourselves by looking either just to the past, or just to the future, we will never be able to "see" ourselves fully. What we lack is an encompassing way of seeing, one that takes in our past at the same time that it opens us up to a new future, beyond the death throes.

A THIRD WAY OF SEEING

Among certain Indian tribes of the South American tropics a story is told that runs, in simple English, something like this:

The fashioner-spirit wanted to give men immortality. To gain it, they must come to the edge of the water. They would see three canoes coming. They must let the first two go on past. In the third canoe would be the spirit of immortality, which the men should greet and welcome.

The first canoe had for cargo a basket of very rotten, reeking meat. The men went toward it but were driven away by the foul smell. The smell told them that this canoe must be carrying death. But in fact death was riding in the second canoe, although in human form. Forgetting their instructions, the men dashed for the second canoe, greeting the form in it.

The third canoe arrived. In it was the promised spirit. But it was now too late. The men had already embraced death. Now they were different from the animals, the trees, the stones, for these all had waited for the arrival of the spirit that gave immortality. If the men had waited, they, too, could throw off their skins, like the snakes, when they grew old, so as to become young again.[7]

Men everywhere have resorted to such stories as a way of understanding self and world, of saying where we came from, why we're the way we are, and what we can hope for. We moderns don't believe such myths, of course. Why not? An easy but wrong answer is that myths don't treat of the real world. But the story we have just looked at talks about men, canoes, and depends entirely on something as earthy as the smell of rotten meat. Moreover, it deals with man's anxiety about himself and his limits, surely a problem at the very heart of the human, real world.

We don't believe in the myth of the three canoes for another reason. It is not *our* myth. We see it from a distance of time, space, and education. It was brought to our attention by a mythologist, who himself "cannot believe in myths because it is his task to pick them to pieces."[8] The word "myth" usually brings to mind someone else's easy-to-put-down story. Thus "myth" becomes something irrelevant or superstitious or fabulous, frozen into archaic statues in museums. Names like Jupiter, Venus, Valhalla, and Beowulf only say to us how out-of-date the subject is.

But there are other, more gripping myths for each man and his community, myths so alive he lives in them, myths so much a part of him that he isn't even aware of them until he stops and thinks about it. These are the ones I want to talk about now—the American myths, the ones *we* live in even as we pick apart primitive stories from the South American rain forest. For we have our own parables of existence, too, our own ways of saying to ourselves who we are, where we came from, why we're the way we are, what's wrong, what can be done about it, and where we hope to be going.

Let me illustrate by taking the liveliest myth I come in daily contact with, living as I do within sight of the Astrodome—the Texas myth. At this writing I have been living in Texas for three years. The deeper, mythical meaning of it did not hit me for well over a year. Then one summer I spent several weeks in France. Always before, when I visited France, I had done so as a Tennessean. This time I went as a Texan. And it made quite a difference.

First of all, I realized I could not really get away from Texas, or the symbols and reminders of it. In Luxembourg City, my first stop, one of the first restaurants I came to was named—what else?—the "Texas." And there was a great map of the state painted on the window, showing three cities: Houston, Dallas, and El Paso.

On the streets of France, I saw dozens of young Europeans wearing western hats. (I was soon sorry I hadn't brought mine along.)

In Reims I had to take my small rented Renault to the local agency for a checkup. The smock-clad technician shook hands and promised to have the car ready the next morning. When I called to pick up the car I was "seen" not as *Monsieur* Sellers, nor as a visiting *professeur*, nor even as an American tourist. I was rather greeted with the cry: "The man from Texas has come for his car."

At the tobacco museum in Bergerac, after I had signed the register, giving my home address, the custodian glanced in the book, saw that I was from Houston, and welcomed me with a mimicked pistol fusillade: "Bang, bang, *monsieur!* Tex-AS, no?"

As I have suggested, all this was rattlingly different from my earlier visits to France. No one then had showed me a map with Memphis or Chattanooga on it. No one was wearing a coonskin cap. No one dreamed of hailing me as "the man from Tennessee." (It is true, however, that a "Nashville" myth with themes and figures drawn from country music is slowly making its way around the world—but it does not yet compare in potency with the Texas myth.) This experience soon led me to believe that there was something about living in Texas that doesn't meet the eye ordinarily, something that isn't found in any empirical observation. There is meaning, *a sense of identity*, even to this day, in the legend of the West, and in the symbolic atmosphere of Texas.

I have made use of the Texas myth not because I think it's the best one around, but because I want to point to a live myth. A myth in the true sense is not a falsehood, a fairy tale, or the superstition of some dead culture. A myth is better defined as a people's way of "seeing" themselves that has the result of transforming them, of giving them a new, saving identity.

How do myths work? Ordinarily by taking over something commonplace in our lives and endowing it with deeper meaning. The most "saving" myths are those that plumb this deeper meaning all the way to the ultimate. Hence the constant presence of gods in the classic myths. Myths connect us, via symbols drawn from everyday reality, with the source of being and meaning. They disclose to us the promise of our beginnings, the hopes of our future, both rescued from the foibles and failures of our errant present time.

Let us take the ordinary Western or Texas hat and consider its mythical properties. First, we need to observe that the Western hat is a piece of everyday reality. It has an ordinary practical function, not mythical at all. As a hat, it shades one's eyes from the sun. Or keeps the rain off. Or protects the pate from the wind.

"Single vision," a term from Blake, taken over recently by Theodore Roszak to describe the insensitivity of scientism, would limit the reality of the hat to this observable level. But the Texas hat has another level of meaning. It not only serves the practical function that any hat serves. It also offers, to anyone who wears it in good faith, a release, *a new identity*, however marginal. It moves him out of one role into another, however slightly; into a freeing role, a role that gives a new outlook on oneself and his future—though it is all fueled, in a sense, with a myth out of the past (in this case the saga of the West and the ordeal of the cowboy).

I said that I chose the Texas myth not because it is the

best of all myths, but because it is a live one. It is far from being the worst of myths, either. Let's compare it for a moment with a competing myth, the "Southern." For much of my life, I lived in the Deep South. For the past few years I have lived in Texas. There is a considerable difference in meaning as between the two experiences. Both modes of existence are shot through, of course, with human finitude, fallibility, and folly. But I see some clear advantages, mythically speaking, to living in Texas.

For one thing, life in the Deep South tended to be a closed society. In some sections of Mississippi or South Carolina or Alabama one almost had to be born there in order to be accounted a full-fledged member of the community. Barring that, one normally had to serve a long while in immigrant status. (I can remember one political office-seeker in my home town actually worrying because the used car he had just bought to campaign in bore license-plate numbers of the next county.)

Texas and the West, for all their sins of other sorts, are different on this matter. One can become a Texan the day he enters the state, if he wishes. That is one of the hidden "identity meanings" of the Texas hat.

The larger question is what mythical identity we might be able to hope for as Americans in the community of nations. True myths offer us a new life, a new deal, a new identity, ultimately a new community. They do so by reminding us of our promise, which means invoking the past, too. They can range from micro-myths that affect us only marginally, through middle-weight myths that change aspects of our identity, to epochal myths that are at the heart of, say, the conversion experiences of the Christian religion, or the meaning of the Covenant with Yahweh in Judaism.

I have found that I have to start off my introductory ethics course at Rice by talking about myth before I ever get to ethics. Most of the students are majors in science or engineering. Yet they yearn, often without knowing it, for the transcendent. There is a technological atmosphere at Rice that is as thick as New Orleans coffee. In such a setting, mythical awareness has been repressed. The result is that too many of us either live in a two-dimensional, flat, mythless world; or else in a jungle world in which strange, untended myths, like weeds, come in and grow crookedly and offer us symbolic tares and toadstools instead of maize and mushrooms. Man is a symbol-using, myth-making creature in his essence, even when he is told that he is not. Our best chance to understand ourselves and our plight, and to recover a sense of community, is to throw open the ports of our mythical awareness, and to cultivate those myths that point us toward a healing, saving change of identity.

MYTH AS NEWS: DEATH AND REBIRTH

Let us imagine ourselves transported to the Australian outback a few decades before the turn of the century. Not far away is a tribe of aborigines. Fortunately we have with us a guide who not only speaks the tribal language, but has made friends with its leaders. He has even learned to fashion and use the bull-roarer, a sacred noise-making device, and the tribesmen have taken him into their confidence. Through his offices we can quietly come into the camp and watch one of their central ceremonies. As we arrive, the ceremony has already started.

The men of the tribe have surrounded the women and children, corralling them, pushing them into a compressed space. Now the old men come in, scrutinize the children, select certain boys. They come to one boy and seem in doubt. The boy himself seems to be in an agony of fright, clinging to his mother. By order of a chieftain he is dragged away. But after a few minutes comes the decision: "He is too young, put him back."

The boys selected are about fourteen or fifteen years old. It is time for them to cease being boys and to become men. Each has been rudely separated from his mother. Now he is stripped naked and wrapped in a blanket. All are led away, up a steep grassy hill, some of the old men in the lead. At the summit comes a magic dance, the first of many rituals and ceremonies. The intent is to fill the boys with the lore of the men who before them had become adults. If the magic takes, then the "spirit from above" will like the new men, and all will be well.

Various ordeals are included. The old men said to one boy that he had played too much with the little girls. A medicine man comes up and as part of a preset ritual, knocks one of his teeth out. The boy is told that he must not spit out the blood. He stands and endures the pain stoically. He is now like the men, who had in their own youth gone through the same religious ritual of the tooth removal.

This is only a sample. The full rite is much longer. Such are the *rites of initiation* of this tribe. The aim is to bring the boy into the tribe, to initiate him into "the whole body of the tribe's mythological and cultural traditions." That is why it all begins with an act of rupture, the taking of the adolescent, sometimes roughly, from his mother. The initiate has to be cut off, for a time, from his past; he must die to it if he is to emerge into a new identity.

The intention of all that is done at this ceremony is to make a momentous change in the boy's life; . . . His connection with his mother as her child is broken off, and he becomes henceforth attached to the men. All the sports and games of his boyhood are to be abandoned with the severance of the old domestic ties between himself and his mother and sisters. He is now to be a man, instructed in and sensible of the duties which devolve upon him as a member of the . . . community.[9]

When we "see" America mythically, a surprising new possibility emerges. Let us turn to this, one of the most persistent elements in any mythology, the practice nearly universal among ancient peoples of rites of initiation (rites of passage, they are also called).

For purposes of argument, let's confine the discussion to the kind of initiation we have just sampled among the Australian tribesmen—the ritual "whose function is to effect the transition from childhood or adolescence to adulthood." This means setting aside other types of initiation, such as "rites for entering a secret society," or the kind of initiation that occurs upon entrance into a mystical vocation. Those are subsidiary to our purpose. We want to explore the meaning of those rites that take us not into secret regions, but into public regions. For that is what "puberty rites" do. They lead into the cultural and spiritual worlds, and into the fullness of one's own being, sexually and otherwise. "It is through initiation," Mircea Eliade says, "that, in primitive and archaic societies, man becomes what he is and what he should be—a being open to the life of the spirit, hence one who participates in the culture into which he was born."[10]

The whole tribe is involved. The rite does not focus purely on the initiates. Although the ceremony has directly in view the entrance of the adolescent into the adult world, there is, for the tribe itself, a movement in the reverse direction: from the present to its own larger rebirth, for "through the repetition, the *reactualization,* of the traditional rites, the entire community is regenerated."[11] Thus the tribe returns to its roots, as it were, to its beginnings at the very same time that the initiate is leaving his own beginnings behind for a new role.

Initiation, as a centerpiece of myth, is just as pertinent to an understanding of twentieth-century Americans and their communities as it was for archaic and primitive peoples. We do not realize it because most of the time we settle for "single vision," and accept conventional historical and scientific accounts of what happens to us. But such accounts always miss the significance, at the mythic level, of the end of an era. A purely historicist explanation of change tends to the view that when someone or something dies, it's gone. A loss is a loss. It's off the screen for good at that point. But the archaic religions understand reality to be a coming and going. Death is joined in twinship with life: one is always followed by the other, in a ceaseless rhythm. Rites of initiation then draw on the imagery of death or destruction to symbolize the cycle of existence, passage from one identity to another, or from an older existence to a new one, from death to rebirth.[12]

"Initiation lies at the core of any genuine human life," says Eliade. We all go through cycles of crisis, suffering, loss of identity, deaths and rebirths of meaning. However satisfying one's life may have been, still we are likely at times to be aware of our failures, and to take the view that we have missed what we had set out to do, or betrayed the best that was in us. "In such moments of total crisis, only one hope seems to offer any issue—the hope of beginning life again. This means, in short, that the man undergoing such a crisis dreams of new, regenerated life, fully realized and significant.[13]

Here is my conviction. I fully accept the evidence of the decline of community in America. But I do not think it adds up to the end. The end of an era, yes. But also the start of something. I believe that America is undergoing, in this crisis of community, a very deep-running *rite of initiation.* It is a movement in both directions. America is an adolescent community ready to die to its recent past so that it may enter, at least a little more, the adult world of nations. And yet, as young as America is, it is also a morally wasted nation at midpassage, which needs to return to its beginnings and to experience a rebirth of what its purpose is all about. What is needed, and what I think is happening to us, is a change of identity. It is part of a process that has been going on for a long time.

Consider the evidence from American history. The main issue between the colonists and Great Britain was not at first the struggle for independence. Instead it was the question of the rights of *Englishmen* to govern themselves. Along with the political revolution, these Englishmen in America experienced a fundamental rite of initiation. Two things happened: the right of self-governance was won, but those who fought for this rite had to give up the identity of "Englishmen" that had been the vehicle in the first place for the idea of self-governance. Now they were not only self-governing, thanks to a revolution, they were Americans, thanks to a rite of passage.

Even this new identity, it soon appeared, was a garment too strait for the expanding human spirit, and further moltings were to be required. Life on the frontier, for example, called for initiation out of the inadequate local loyalties that had developed on the Eastern seaboard. The frontiersmen found themselves with a new national awareness—the same awareness, we might add, that has been making such heavy weather of it today.

The most painful initiation in American history, so far, has been the Civil War, when old notions of who was an American had to be slain, and new ones (imperfectly) born. After that rupture and rebirth, the country took on new roles and an identity that persisted down through the 1960's: America as technological hero in victorious struggle over nature, and America as something like father figure, politically, for the rest of the world. Our current time of disarray, unease, and failure of community means that this older identity once more is to be replaced.

RUPTURE AND RENEWAL: AN OLD THEME

This theme of death and rebirth was a favorite of the American revivalist preachers back in the Great Awakening. If you yearn to know the joy of a new life, they had preached, then you must recognize, with a kind of merciless realism, how unsatisfactory your present life is. (It's a plea not limited to revivalists: the alcoholic, for example, under most regimens of treatment, must come to exactly the same terms with himself.) "By the ... discoveries of danger, misery, and helplessness," Jonathan Edwards had preached, "the heart is prepared to embrace a discovery of mercy." At that point, once realism sets in, "The gospel then, if it be heard spiritually, will be glad tidings indeed; the most joyful ... ever heard."[14]

This old revivalism, which I, along with hosts of other sophisticates, humanists, and liberals, was once prepared to see permanently shelved, really dovetails quite well with our discoveries about the pertinence of *initiation* in human life. Death throes, properly apprehended, intimate new life. New life springs out of the old, out of passage across a river of trauma. The secret of life requires giving up those fond illusions that only brought us to grief before. What is required, however, is an "act of rupture." What went before must resolutely be seen as failure; what is to come must earnestly be grasped as a new opportunity.

To share in the "rites of passage" from old community to new in America, then, means full recognition of the difficulties we now face. And it must be more than a description of surface symptoms, which is about as far as we got in Chapter I ("The Death Throes"). What we must now undertake is to see how the "warming fires" of community in America, the sponsoring value-clusters, have themselves faded. What is needed, before we can go on to talk of the renewal of community, is a hard-headed inventory of our recent failures, ethically speaking, at keeping the fires going.

IV

A Hard-Headed Inventory

Davy Crockett was frontier America's favorite hero. An actual person (bear hunter, Tennessee Congressman, defender of the Alamo), he caught the fancy of his fellows, and they transformed him into an epic folklore figure, a rip-roaring, legendary, superhuman frontiersman.

There is one gaping flaw in the myth of Davy Crockett. It does tell us what great frontier-conquerers we Americans are, and it does comfort us that plain, homespun manners are as good as anybody else's. But it neglects to tell us another thing about ourselves: that pure conquest is not enough to make us new men.

The Davy Crockett of the ancient Near East was a Sumerian hero figure called Gilgamesh. He, too, is a giant-killer. But this story goes a step beyond that of Davy Crockett: it reckons with the inner man, and with the need, as we now put it, to take a hard-headed inventory of ourselves.

Like Davy Crockett, Gilgamesh seems originally to have been a real historical figure. King of Uruk, a Babylonian city, he was a remarkable builder, having put up a colossal wall around his city. This and other exploits grew in stories, and Gilgamesh became thought of as "two-thirds god, one-third man."

Early on in the epic, Gilgamesh gets into a fight with a man named Enkidu. In a notable un-Davylike development, Enkidu wins! Gilgamesh and Enkidu become fast friends, even so, and they decide to go out to the distant forest and take on the dread monster Khumbaba, whose "bellow is a stormwind," whose "mouth is fire," whose "snort is death."

Gradually we begin to suspect that Enkidu is really Gilgamesh's alter ego, his better self. Gilgamesh is bent on physical conquest. Enkidu is more thoughtful, given over to introspection. That suspicion helps us to see why the elders, when the two leave on their conquest, give this advice:

"Gilgamesh, trust not in thy powers. . . . Let Enkidu go on before thee, . . . He is wise in fight, he understandeth combats."[1]

The two friends, with the help of a friendly god, succeed in dispatching the monster, and they return to the city. The bubble of success now bursts. Enkidu takes sick and dies. Gilgamesh is distraught that his partner, "panther of the slopes," with whom he has laid lions low and slain monsters, is gone. Then comes another feeling. It is not just a question of grieving for Enkidu. Gilgamesh is now gripped by a more self-serving emotion—every man for himself:

"Will I too not die as Enkidu? . . .
I have gotten the fear of death."[2]

But perhaps there is a way out. Gilgamesh has heard of a distant figure, Utnapishtim, who outwitted death in the great flood (here the tale shows kinship with the biblical story of Noah). He will find his way to him.

After arduous travels Gilgamesh arrives at water's edge. There a divine barmaid (or seer) warns him he will have to cross these, the very waters of death. She directs him to Ur-Shanabi, the ferryman. After a narrow escape, and after breaking all of their oars, the two accomplish the great feat of crossing the dread river.

Utnapishtim, the wise old man, receives Gilgamesh, but takes a dim view of him, doubts that he is fit to know the secret of life. Utnapishtim's wife, who is very much a part of the action, talks her husband into giving Gilgamesh a chance.

Immediately there is a bad sign. The couple put Gilgamesh to sleep so that he may dream saving knowledge. He sleeps seven nights. When he wakes up, he has dreamed nothing, indeed thinks he has only slept a moment.

In the language of initiation, Gilgamesh is simply not yet ready to cross the threshold and enter the new life.

Nevertheless, he is a persistent fellow, and he finally learns from the old man just what the secret of life is. In the deep, there is a plant with thorns. "If thy hands will obtain that plant, thou wilt find new life." Resourceful in doing and making, Gilgamesh ties weights to his feet and descends. He grasps the wonderful plant, though the thorns hurt. Joyfully he announces his find to the ferryman: "This plant is a wondrous plant, . . . Its name is 'The old man becomes young as the man in his prime.' I myself will eat it that I may return to my youth."[3]

But when Gilgamesh went to a pool to bathe, a serpent saw the plant, came out of the water, snatched and ate it. Gilgamesh sat and wept. He has worn himself out—and for nothing.

Why did he fail? He still sees things in self-serving terms. He wants immortality, but only for himself, and he has a shallow idea even of that, wanting to live on "only in the outward physical sense."[4] The inwardness, in new spirit, the joy in others' lives that go with rebirth have escaped him.

At the very end, after he has failed, Gilgamesh seems at last aware of what he is lacking. At this point he may be ready, for the first time, for rebirth.

We Americans, I fear, have fallen into the same trap that Gilgamesh did. Beguiled by conquest and success, we have lost that inner sense of what community should be. Frightened by old age and death, we yearn for biological prolongation of life rather than rebirth of common spirit. All this is nowhere more clear than in the hardening and loss of meaning that have befallen those three ethics clusters.

What we need is a hard-headed inventory of ourselves and of our eroding moral resources in the hope that we, too, may become aware of our failures, and at an earlier point than Gilgamesh, who woke up to himself when it was too late.

WHATEVER BECAME OF THE RIGHTEOUSNESS ETHIC?

I hadn't been in Houston long before I heard from Chuck Houseman, a former theology student at Vanderbilt, now associate minister of a fashionable Protestant church in the western suburbs. Could I come out and speak? Having been involved in thinking through the themes that I am discussing here, I suggested we take up the changing role of work in America—how the young among us, for example, were pushing for a new scenario that prizes the value of "sitting around and being" as much as striving, working, and doing.

To get things going, I began with a sketch of the plot of a turn-of-the-century Horatio Alger novel, *Adrift in New York*. In this story, the hero of course begins in rags and winds up rich, having put down the scheming scoundrel and won the beautiful girl. All of this, I had supposed, would come across as amusing. After all, it was a dated, campy tale. Its morality was dubious. The plot itself was stitched together by ridiculous coincidences.

Except for one trendy matron, hardly anyone even smiled. Instead, a serious discussion set in. Since that's what I had come for, I couldn't complain.

The teen-agers there had only been reminded by the melodramatic story of how behind the times, in their view, our society still is.

Another group put in a spirited good word for the work ethic.

What surprised me was the intensity with which all hands focused on the issue of *work*. Those who spoke for a new ethic were just as effectively riveted there as those who wanted to support the old ethic. There is nothing wrong with advocating work; there is nothing wrong with advocating that we not work some of the time. What concerns me is the tendency to define virtue, in either case, in terms of work. Indeed, we have almost reached the point of tying questions of our very identity to the work we do.

A young man attending a theological conference on technology tells the story of the time he decided to do nothing for a certain period of time. He had enough money for the moment, he wasn't going to school, so he simply existed, rather than worked. Of religious bent, he attended a wealthy suburban church. The minister

asked him what he did. He replied: "I'm unemployed."
One woman even thought to introduce him to a young
woman his age. Visibly dismayed, she did it this way:
"This is Mr. Brewster. He is unemployed, but he still
seems very nice."

Reflected Mr. Brewster: "That woman put into one
sentence a whole volume of values that she . . . upholds.
Well, . . . some of these have to go."[5]

I have no quarrel with work. What I do want to question is our tendency to equate it with the sum and substance of the Puritan ethic. This is to leave out the heart
of the matter, to lose the genuine meaning of the Puritan venture for righteousness in America.

How could we end up here? For the Puritan
theologian Jonathan Edwards, the original motif of the
righteousness ethic was of a will inwardly changed by
the love of God. This rightened will, it was supposed,
would move toward community-strengthening acts. By
now, the inwardness of this ethic has been almost entirely lost. Its power to support community has been lost
to exactly the same degree.

What is left is a collection of sayings, dogmas, moral
slogans, and thoughts for the day that no longer corre-
spond to anything about the condition of our wills, or to
the notion of "benevolence to being." Rather, they seek
to justify affluence, the status quo, and the lot of the fortunate.

As far back as the turn of the century, the heirs of the
righteousness ethic were already having to scramble
about to find plausible moral reasons for justifying
work, property, and wealth. Andrew Carnegie, a captain of the steel industry and philanthropist, wrote one
of the most convincing arguments, and was a leader in a
movement that seemed to put new vitality into the
righteousness ethic—now in the form of the "Gospel of
Wealth." But to make his case Carnegie had to turn the

original Puritan ethic upside down. Instead of seeing achievement, and thus wealth, as a *sign* of a right will, Carnegie seems to argue that wealth is what enables a man to move to a good will!

Let us follow his argument briefly as it appears in his famous essay, "Wealth," published in 1889 in the *North American Review*. To begin with, Carnegie sees no moral problem in the acquisition of wealth by the few. That is inevitable, and a good thing in the bargain. The problem lies almost entirely in what is to be done with the wealth of those who, with their superior talents, do acquire it.

Wealth comes according to the inexorable laws of human nature and civilization, says Carnegie. These include the law of competition and survival of the fittest: "It is here; we cannot evade it; no substitutes for it have been found." These laws also include the right of property, upon the "sacredness" of which civilization itself depends—"the right of the laborer to his hundred dollars in the savings bank, and equally the legal right of the millionaire to his millions." Finally, these laws include individualism. Even if we were to try to change them, and substitute an allegedly "nobler ideal that man should labor, not for himself alone, but in and for a brotherhood of his fellows," we would only create chaos. This would be "revolution," an attempt to change human nature itself ("a work of aeons").

In sum, the present industrial system, based on these axioms—survival of the fittest, property, and individualism—assures us "a condition of affairs under which the best interests of the race are promoted." This is true even though the effect is inevitably to give wealth to the few. As we can see here, the accumulation of wealth is no longer even claimed, by one of its most gifted American interpreters, to flow from a right will. It flows, rather, from the competitive drive, the fight to survive, zeal for property, and every man's right to work for "himself alone" instead of for the group.

But good will does enter the picture for Carnegie. What is the wealthy man to do with his millions? Instead of leaving his money to his heirs, or even leaving it for public purposes, Carnegie argues, the rich man ought to administer his surplus wealth during his own lifetime. And he ought to make his end the good of his fellow men. The Carnegie Libraries in dozens of American cities are evidence that Carnegie took this thesis seriously in distributing his own wealth.

Presumably, the man of wealth has had a good will all the time. But it was not needed for acquiring the wealth. Now, after the wealth is in hand, the combative faculties are to be leashed, and good will brought forward. Carnegie sums up:

This, then, is held to be the duty of the man of Wealth: First, to set an example of modest, unostentatious living, shunning display or extravagance; to provide moderately for the legitimate wants of those dependent on him; and after doing so to consider all surplus revenues which come to him simply as trust funds, which he is called upon to administer . . . in the manner . . . best calculated to produce the most beneficial results for the community.[6]

Carnegie's "man of wealth" becomes the agent of the poor, serving them through his superior talents, "doing for them better than they would or could do for themselves." In spite of the moral dubiety of this position —wealth acquired by aggressiveness, dispensed by paternalism—there is something to be said for it. Carnegie does at least articulate a thesis of *obligation to community,* belated in the rich man's life cycle though it may be. And the country is doubtless better off for the philanthropies of its Carnegies, Mellons, Fords, Rockefellers. At the same time, let us note that the original

basis for community that we discerned in the righteousness ethic has been overturned. Wealth has become the
enabler of good will rather than the outcome of it. With
this reversal, community surely suffers, no matter how
many fortunes are visited upon us by men in their
counting houses.

I wish I could say I thought we were doing better
today. But the situation, I fear, is worse. More of us are
better off financially, and by Carnegie's theory more of
us should thus be serving our communities. Not that
millionaires are so common, but affluence, with its potential for discretionary spending, is widespread in the
middle class. The result is more often than not to draw
the line even more sharply between "us" and "them."
This is no way to say "we." It is to fall in the same trap as
Gilgamesh.

A few months ago, a Houston reporter, one of the
new breed of muckrakers, did a series on the kind of
working conditions experienced in well-to-do neighborhoods by black maids. Here we'll take up one case
—the situation of a maid whom we'll call Ollie Nicholas.

Mrs. Nicholas has to get up before daylight, fix breakfast for her two children, leave them watching television, lock the front door, and walk two blocks to catch
her bus. Downtown, she has to transfer. After the second bus ride, she still has to walk three blocks. "We'll
pick you up on rainy days," the woman of the house had
said. But Mrs. Nicholas knows from sad experience that
she cannot count on it.

Inside, she faces a kitchen full of someone else's dirty
dishes, and a day's work. "I'll be late tonight," says the
woman of the house. "Probably half an hour." Which
means probably an hour. Since there are children to be
minded, Mrs. Nicholas must stay. She will miss the last
of the frequent buses, so she won't get home to her own
children until about 7:30.

Pay day comes. She waits to be paid. "Your money—I forgot. Didn't get to the bank today. Well, you don't mind waiting until Monday, do you?"[7]

Quite apart from issues the justice ethic would raise—racial, economic, and women's rights—we see here the low estate of the remnants of the righteousness ethic. The devolution from Carnegie's Gospel of wealth is obvious. For here there is little sense of obligation to the other in community.

So far we have talked mostly about work, wealth, economic factors. We can see the same sort of breakdown and hardening if we look at the religious scene in America today. One of the saddest examples is the way the Bible has been transformed, from an inward word that could judge us, transform us, overjoy us, into a clumsily read manual of pseudo-history and pseudo-geography. The results are appalling and often laughable.

Amercans of all faiths have tended to interpret the Bible more woodenly than their European forebears. Why? I'm not sure. I suspect it's because we're further away in culture, time, and space from the biblical origins. European culture flourished over great ages of faith, when the biblical teachings were part of the culture itself. The settlement of America, for the most part, followed these great ages of faith. Perhaps the Puritans, with their "Bible Commonwealth," were the exception, for the spirit of religious culture lived with them for a while. By and large, however, the Bible came to America as an input from a previous culture; we weren't as close to it as the Europeans. So we have always tended to interpret it less existentially, more woodenly. Literal interpretations of the Bible have existed on both sides of the Atlantic, of course. But European religious orthodoxy has always been more complex, subtle, and profound than American fundamentalism. Luther and Calvin were "orthodox" theologians and "literalists." But the Bible, for them, was to be heard inwardly. It was the message of man's confrontation by God, God's judgment upon him, God's joyous promise to him.

When the Bible is seen with "single vision," taken only literally, it loses its power to speak inwardly. In fact, it becomes the captive of exploitation. In Blountstown, Florida, not far from where I used to live, there was a real estate agent who advertised that the Florida panhandle was actually the original "Garden of Eden," and that God created Adam "one mile east of Bristol, Florida." America has seen spectacular new amusement parks—Disneyland, Astroworld, Six Flags. Running parallel to this phenomenon is the emergence of amusement projects devoted to Bible and "Holy Land" themes—another dubious fruit of America's commercial zeal married with wooden understanding of scripture. The *New York Times* reports one such project, a $30,000,000 venture undertaken by "a group of religious-minded men" for Southeast Ohio. "Biblelands," as it was to be called, would include camel rides, real fish and fishing in a "Sea of Galilee," and excursions to the "land of milk and honey." There was to be a display of wax religious figures, and theatrical productions. The project was to be built near the world's largest freeway interchange, at the intersection of Interstates 70 and 77. Fittingly, the opening ceremonies were set for 1976 , the year of our American bicentennial. In Florida, not far from Disney World, tourists will be offered the inspirations of "Bible World," a walled city funded at $11,000,000 and designed to transport one magically into the ambience of biblical Jerusalem. Visitors will find not only puppets enacting the story of David and Goliath, they can also participate in a Bible quiz show and buy Persian rugs.[8]

What does it mean? American religion, having lost the inwardness of the right-will ethic, now looks to the Bible in an inflexible, wooden fashion. The result is to rob the message of its deeper meaning. Instead of pointing us to the acts of contrition and commitment that could underwrite community, this new American religiosity offers us ultimately an escape from that judgment.

In or out of the churches, self-righteousness is one of the sorriest attributes among defenders of the status quo. Little clues to it are often the most revealing—such as the slogans posted from time to time on the outdoor-advertising signs of churches, insurance agencies, and real estate dealers. Near Rice stadium there is an insurance office that I pass every time I walk to the bank. I am always interested in seeing if there is a new punch line. Here is the latest one:

"Take your duties more seriously and your rights less so."

That slogan is a commentary, I think, on the plight of community in America. To be sure, it is an admirable thing to extol the doing of one's duty. But need one's rights thereby be disparaged? Need such a line be drawn in the dust? Finally, at the extremity of its distortion, the worn-out righteousness ethic becomes a battering ram, a tool of non-community, a flying wedge aimed at the rights, and hence the moral basis for living, of the others.

But, as we shall see, something of the same is true of each of the other worn-out ethics, also.

FROM THOMAS JEFFERSON TO JEB STUART MAGRUDER

Testifying before television cameras to the Senate committee investigating the political scandals of 1972-3, the witness with the choir-boy eyes didn't exactly put the blame on his old ethics teacher, back at Williams College. But he came close, all the same.

Jeb Stuart Magruder had been deputy director of the Republicans' 1972 committee for the re-election of the president. He was telling what he knew of the Watergate affair, which came to light when burglars, with committee funds in their pockets, were apprehended inside the Democratic National Committee headquarters in Washington's Watergate complex.

Magruder, it was becoming apparent, had been in on the plotting, and took part in later efforts to cover up the affair.

Now, toward the end of his testimony, Magruder was cross-examined by Senator Howard Baker. Interested in the witness' moral perceptions, Baker asked Magruder why he had become involved in improper and illegal actions.

Magruder, in effect, gave two reasons.

First, there was the overwhelming importance of getting the president elected to a second term. The president's team was so loyal to him, so zealous for his future, that they were willing to break the rules. Their end was so important, they thought, that such actions were justified.

Second, Magruder's one-time ethics teacher at Williams College, the Rev. William Sloan Coffin, after all, had himself engaged in acts of civil disobedience in the course of protests against the Vietnamese war. Although "two wrongs don't make a right," Magruder conceded, still, if the enemies of the administration could break the law, and even justify it by ethical reasoning, why couldn't the president's campaigners do the same?

Magruder's former teacher, by now chaplain at Yale, didn't, of course, buy Magruder's logic.

"There was not very much on civil disobedience in the

ethics course I taught," Coffin commented after Magruder had testified, "so poor old Jeb never learned to tell the difference between civil disobedience and violations of the Constitution by the Administration."[8]

Magruder's remarks on ethics set off an editorial controversy. The *Christian Science Monitor* severely criticized Magruder. The *Wall Street Journal* supported him, up to a point.

The *Monitor* was troubled by the easy way in which Magruder identified Watergate wrongdoings with "Mr. Coffin's sort of antiwar civil disobedience." Coffin did engage in protests. But, as he explained, his protests were aimed at testing the constitutionality of a law. In some cases the only way one can do that is not to obey the law. Besides, said Coffin, "we didn't try to infringe the civil liberties of anyone. Magruder and his folks were deliberately violating those liberties."[9]

But the *Wall Street Journal* found Magruder's explanation plausible. After all, many kinds of civil disobedience were occurring in those days. Not that there weren't differences among them: "There is an important distinction to be drawn between unethical and illegal activities of private citizens, even professors of ethics, and clandestine activities by the government itself." When governments engage in illegal acts, they are assulting the very moral foundations of society.

Still, said the *Journal,* "Those in the worst position to condemn the lawbreaking at Watergate are those who themselves previously counseled lawlessness and disobedience in the name of higher authority." Some of the antiwar protesters and civil rights workers of the recent past, it granted, did practice civil disobedience in exemplary fashion, "following their consciences to jail." But as time went on, the movement lost its idealism; many of its spokesmen, pressed to the wall, seemed to lose interest in high principle, choosing to raise legal technicalities as a means of staying out of jail, "even if this left the moral point clouded." The *Journal* cited the case of the Berrigan brothers, priests who led a cirle of Catholic draft resisters. This group was charged with raiding Selective Service offices and mutilating draft files "by such dramatic devices as soaking them with duck's blood."

By the end of their trial, said the *Journal,* "Fathers Daniel and Philip and several co-defendants decided not to accept their punishment and went on the lam."

All in all, concludes the *Journal,* the history of this movement indicates that "civil disobedience quickly degenerates into a general spirit of lawlessness, and that in such an atmosphere the law loses some of its authority as a guide to public behavior." Perhaps this sequence of illegal acts did, indeed, set the state for the "all but inevitable next step in this degeneration," the "equally lawless repression from the men in charge of Watergate."[10]

It might help if we introduce a clear, valid definition of civil disobedience. In a thoughtful recent study, James F. Childress finds three elements that must be present if such acts are to meet his criteria for acts of valid civil disobedience:

First, the act must be *public* rather than clandestine.

Second, the act must be *nonviolent* rather than violent.

Third, the act must be, as a test involving breaking of the law, *submissive* rather than evasive. That is, the doer of the act, instead of attempting to flee, "will submit to arrest and punishment."[11]

If we define civil disobedience in this fashion (and I find Childress reasonable and persuasive on the subject), then it is a gross error to equate it with "Watergate" style activities, such as burglary, electronic bugging, forgery of cables and letters, and the like.

And yet we cannot completely dismiss the *Wall Street*

Journal position. For not all activities claimed to be civil disobedience have met the Childress criteria. Nor can we entirely dismiss Jeb Stuart Magruder's juxtaposition of his own activities with those of civil disobedience—as facile and self-serving as his remarks may have been.

Let's go back for a moment to the justice-dissent ethic as we examined it earlier, in the words and deeds of Thomas Jefferson and Abraham Lincoln.[12] We might recall two special features of this ethic:

First, it values law less than does the righteousness ethic as a way of opening up community.

Second, it values goals in the future, some of them still unfolding, instead of concentrating upon the status quo.

This ethic, for these two reasons, has a built-in ambiguity. It may produce sound, defensible modes of protest, such as civil disobedience of the sort practiced by Martin Luther King, Jr., and many others. Because of its relativism and futurism, however, this ethic can also produce less desirable progeny. One of them is, of course, the more risky, seamy, and violent forms of protest. The justice ethic can also produce, in the name of progress, another dubious offspring that I will call, for want of a better name, *the expediency ethic.*

"What an enormous premium you must place on success!" exclaimed a stupefied Senator Baker to Magruder's boss, former campaign manager John Mitchell, after Mitchell hinted he had condoned illegal acts, so anxious was he to see the president re-elected.[13]

Where did Magruder and Mitchell learn their ethics? Not from proponents of civil disobedience as carefully defined above. They learned their ethics, or non-ethics, from the degenerate tradition in this country that values progress, success, "getting things done" above all else. They adopted the expediency ethic.

It is the same kind of transition we have followed in

the righteousness ethic: from a transformed will to its very opposite, self-righteousness. Here we see a transition from hope in the future to making sure, at any cost, that a certain future is realized. The expediency ethic has threatened, like a crop of weeds, to choke out the legitimate plants in the garden of justice.

There are important nineteenth-century transitions in the justice ethic that show us what was on the way.

On the one hand, we find earnest voices raised to pass along the torch of the justice ethic in its full dimensions. In the same era when Andrew Carnegie was speaking out for the "Gospel of Wealth," such critics of economic injustice as Walter Rauschenbusch, a Baptist clergyman of German extraction, were arguing for the "Social Gospel." In Rauschenbusch's eyes, it was still possible to distinguish clearly between justice and expediency.

"The spirit of primitive Christianity did not spread only sweet peace and tender charity," Rauschenbusch said, "but the leaven of social unrest." It awakened slaves. It aroused workers. It stirred subjects of the state. It fostered in all "a sense of worth and a longing for freedom."

Now, in the day of economic exploitation of working men, Rauschenbusch argued, we can do no less than continue this protest. This means opposing the standing order. "In practice law and order are on the side of those in possession. The men who are out can get in only through the disturbance of the order now prevailing. Those who in the past cried for law and order at any cost have throttled many a new-born child of justice."[14]

This was the "Social Gospel," and its proponents had much to do with changing the plight of the working man in America from one of underprivilege to relative affluence.

Still, there is a loose end, a nagging doubt, one that we

have already encountered. If the future is more important than the present, it is easy to be tempted. It is not a large step from dissent to pragmatism and from there to opportunism. It is not a large step from hope in the future to insistence, at any cost, on "progress" and "success."

How closely related justice and the pragmatic spirit can be is well shown in the work of a famous American philosopher, John Dewey, whose thought, like that of Rauschenbusch, leads from the nineteenth into the twentieth century.

Dewey saw himself as standing squarely within the tradition we have called here the justice ethic. The main purpose of society, he says, "is to set free and to develop the capacities of human individuals without respect to race, sex, class or economic status."

How does this purpose get to be realized? By forward movement, by change, by problem solving, by growth. If democracy has any "moral meaning," says Dewey, it is found in the contribution it and its institutions make "to the all-around growth of every member of society."

Moral goods and ends exist only when something has to be done. The fact that we have not yet arrived, that we do still have community problems, only shows that there are "deficiencies, evils in the existent situation." For moving forward, what are our criteria? How do we know we are moving properly? First, let us rid ourselves of false criteria. Morality, says Dewey, "is not a catalogue of acts nor a set of rules to be applied like drugstore prescriptions or cook-book recipes."[15]

At this point, Dewey and Rauschenbusch are on divergent courses. Rauschenbusch's futurism is informed by a high religious ideal: the biblical notion of the Kingdom of God, in which injustice and economic privation will be overcome. For Dewey, however, such lofty principles are irrelevant or actually harmful.

For Dewey, in fact, there are no fixed intrinsic values. And so at this point, if Dewey speaks for the future, we say goodbye to: *the right will,* good in itself—the intrinsic value of the righteousness ethic; *the "rights of man"* of the justice ethic—set in a religious context by the Social Gospel; and even *the salvific personal relationships* of the encounter ethic—if they are not geared to problem-solving.

Not that Dewey or pragmatic philosophy was opposed to any of these values. The point is that they all come to be defined in a new way now. They can no longer be seen as prior, pre-existent, intrinsic values, giving life to community. On the contrary, the ongoing life of the community is now what gives meaning to such values. "So-called intrinsic goods, whether religious or esthetic," says Dewey, "are divorced from those interests of daily life which form the preoccupation of the great mass."[16]

If there are no intrinsic values, no fixed ends, what do we look to? "Growing, or the continuous reconstruction of experience, is the only end." From here it is not far to the familiar ethic of aggressiveness that begins at last to seem so counterproductive in our own day. Dewey, in this sequence of ideas, has been insisting all along on an "active conception of knowledge," in which man defines and changes his environment. If this way of knowing prevails, he says, "and the environment is regarded as something that has to be changed in order to be truly known, men are imbued with courage, with what may also be termed an aggressive attitude toward nature."[17]

Dewey was a distinguished philosopher, dedicated to the welfare of human community. However it may have been used by others, Dewey did not intend his philosophy as an "expediency ethic." Moreover, the justice ethic can still be heard from today, but its voice is more and more drowned out by a reductionistic, utility ethic of expediency—the exact analogue to biblical literalism in the devolution of the righteousness ethic.

Every advance in the field of human rights seems to carry with it the risk that it will fray at the edges into expediency. In a biting critique that steps on toes in all directions, Nick Thimmesch speaks of the perils of "the abortion culture," which, in the name of usefulness and human rights, has brought with it a "creeping utilitarian ethic." It can be used to justify terrifying liberties with human life. "In one operating room, surgeons labor to save a 21-week-old baby; in the next, surgeons destroy, by abortion, another child, who can also be reckoned to be 21 weeks old." Thimmesch takes on the eugenicists. In Nazi Germany, mental patients were killed in the name of eugenics. Can we be sure that will not happen to us? In the United States, he adds, pro-abortionists now also serve in pro-euthanasia organizations. "Sorry, but I see a pattern." There are other horrors. "Utilitarians ran the experiment in which syphilitic black men died through lack of penicillin."[18]

Not all of us would agree to lump together abortion, euthanasia and such experiments. We would want to take each issue on its merits. Some of us would justify early abortions on grounds of women's rights. Others would justify some forms of euthanasia. Few thoughtful people would justify withholding medication from diseased illiterates. Still, Thimmesch's point is not overcome by such caveats. Indeed, the fact that we differ so widely about the dangers of such matters only proves his point, in a way: it shows how each of us, in the name of justice and human rights, cuts the cloth to suit himself.[19]

How the justice ethic has declined can be seen if we glance briefly at the changing fortunes of the working man and the black man, two of this ethic's historic sources of concern.

If the working man has become more affluent today,

that is all to the good. At the same time, it is a bit disillusioning to notice what affluence does to the sense of injustice. When the "hard hats" of the construction industry opposed student and black demonstrators a few years ago, the meaning was unmistakeable: organized labor is now a sustaining member, along with capital, management, and computer, of the system. Insofar as he has become emancipated himself from poverty and industrial oppression, the working man has tended to leave dissent and the cry for justice to others. The familiar split between haves and have-nots is no longer understandable as a capital vs. labor cleavage. It can be, and often is, labor haves vs. labor have-nots, as when the well-entrenched and funded Teamsters union clashed with the more proletarian grape workers' organization headed by Cesar Chavez in California.[20]

The civil rights movement, following the murder of Martin Luther King, Jr., was plagued by dissension, failing morale, and diminished support, financial and moral.

"Every black leader I see is trying to get rich himself," offered the Rev. Ralph D. Abernathy, King's successor as president of the Southern Christian Leadership Conference. "They are so full of trickery and trying to get in the headlines, in the magazines, or on the cover of *Time*." He said he saw few black leaders around with enough "integrity and honesty" to get out in front of the movement.[21]

As with the working man, to the extent that the black man's lot has improved, that is a gain rather than a decline. And there have been gains, in income, education, access to public places, implementation of rights. In the cities and in the South, particularly, blacks have begun to exert political power; many of the white Southern politicians now emerging seem to have left racism behind.

But the truth is that the march toward justice, for the

black man, has slowed down alarmingly. Since 1968, according to a University of Michigan study, black distrust of the government grew four times faster than among whites.[22] Old patterns of grouping and culture persist, and continue to victimize blacks. Ghettoes still exist in the big cities. A black resident of New York City is still eight times more likely to be murdered than a white living there.[23] Predominantly black schools are still not good enough. Blacks still cannot purchase homes in most suburban neighborhoods.

So the *need* for a justice ethic is still there, as much as ever. But it is the day of the expediency ethic, when good intentions and bad get hopelessly mixed together, and good intentions like Leo Durocher's "nice guys," tend to finish last. In Galveston, a football coach (white) was fired for tampering with the records of a black player so the player could be accepted for admission by the University of Oklahoma. Later, when the tampering was discovered, the Oklahoma team was forced to forfeit eight games from its past championship season.

Why did the coach do it? Ironically, he echoed the words of Martin Luther King, Jr. "I did it for the player. It gave him a chance to *be somebody.*"[24]

As things stand, the historic justice-dissent ethic in America has been threatened, and upstaged, by an expediency ethic in which, seemingly, almost anything goes. Even the remaining practitioners of the valid justice ethic, honorable and legitimate in their dissents, have slowed down, turned aside. The demonstrations, both good and bad, have tapered off. The students of late have been studying again, riding their bicycles, and sitting quietly under the trees. That is surely not all bad, but it cannot be entirely healthy, either. The civil rights movement, as we have seen, has contracted, its forces dispersed, some of its organizations leaderless. Labor, long the muscle of the justice forces, tends to defect to the status quo.

It is perhaps futile even to try to resurrect the justice-dissent ethic in vintage form. Some profess to see a ray of hope in such catastrophes as Watergate, on the supposition that airing the mess could help the country "restore the place of moral questioning and ethical conduct in public life."[25] Perhaps so—if the recognition of failure here is genuine.

One thing is certain. Community in America is crippled when this historic base of its future, the justice ethic, is debased.

THE RISE AND FALL OF THE YOUTH REVOLUTION

Two notable "rock festivals," only a few years apart, each a temporary mecca for thousands upon thousands of American youth, offer an instructive contrast.

The first was "Woodstock." (The name comes from the place in New York where it was held.) Woodstock came in 1969, at the end of a decade in which the younger generation made a spirited struggle to have its say about American society, and seemed to be making its mark on American community. It was, according to its defenders, a massive communal experience. Rock bands, marijuana, nude bathing—these were all accessories to what happened. The real point about Woodstock was its testimony to the spirit of free souls gathering *en masse* and sharing a vision of what American community should be.

Four years later came "Watkins Glen," also named for its New York location (160 miles west of Woodstock). This time the largest crowd of all came: a swarming anthill of more than half a million youth. Like Woodstock it drew attendants who wanted to hear the music and feel the "vibes" of communion with like-minded lovers of peace. Like Woodstock there was pot and nudity (fewer hard drugs this time, probably more booze). Like

Woodstock the kids were mostly well behaved, though many had been stoned and an unbelievable mountain of garbage was left behind.

But there was also a difference. Woodstock had been, for many Americans, a credible statement by the youth generation about community, and even politicians would have to take it seriously. Watkins Glen was something less. The inner meaning of it all had disappeared. In the words of a twenty-three-year-old Californian who had driven across the country to be there: "It's a party, man, that's all it is." A reporter summed it up as "the biggest nonpolitical event in the Western world."

By the 1970's the spirit of the youth revolution had subsided, and a notable attempt to influence American community in the direction of the encounter ethic had fallen short. I have been asking myself why this attempt failed. It is once again, I fear, the familiar problem of an ethical stance losing its inner meaning, and of its adherents succumbing to externals. (Again, the parallel to Gilgamesh is striking.)

Perhaps we can see what was happening if we examine briefly one of the ethical movements associated with, and widely relied on by the youth movements of the 1960's. Just as the righteousness ethic took on new life from Carnegie's "Gospel of Wealth," just as the justice ethic took on new life from Rauschenbusch's "Social Gospel," so the encounter ethic some years later received a new formulation and head of steam. I am thinking of a movement called both "the New Morality" and "Situation Ethics," which was widely taken as the moral guideline for those who wished to focus on the quality of human relationships.

Practiced both within communes and among citizens at large, this new ethics stance could be seen as taking up the struggle waged earlier by John Humphrey Noyes. Devotees of "the New Morality" certainly weren't classical perfectionists. But they did seek new, honest relationships, love without legalism. They relied on the capacity to care, no matter what moral codes say, and thus they, as much as Noyes and his followers, behaved as though the Kingdom of Heaven were at hand.

True enough, its practitioners weren't always clear just what "the New Morality" meant—except that it had to do with freed-up relations. Sometimes it seemed to mean mainly a new, relaxed attitude toward sex. Sometimes it seemed to mean something downright negative—revolt against yesterday's guidelines to behavior, outright rejection of all hard-and-fast rules of conduct, even a kind of anger at the past, and a contempt for history. And yet it also meant a new moral intensity among the young in our society, especially those concerned with peace, intimacy, and dialogue.

To capture the mood of the youth-generation morality, we have to use gentle words like openness, honesty, candor, and casualness. But we also have to include a countermotif of hostile phrases: radical alienation, impatience with pretense, rejection of custom and convention and even good manners, anger at phoniness and fraud. Finally we have to note a remarkable concern for resonance at least with one's immediate neighbors and sometimes with those far away, and a striking degree of personal availability to one's companions.

The extinct "Free Speech" movement at the University of California at Berkeley probably best illustrated this tendency toward openness and candor. Among the really serious devotees of the movement, this attitude took—and takes, for it still has devotees—the form of a headstrong insistence that men and women may, and must, show their feelings, without guilt. Its devotees go on, like their forebears in the encounter-ethic tradition, to insist that deep personal relationships are the substance of salvation, the medicine of immortality. As a corollary it was added that bodily propinquity is a sacramental expression of this salvation, that what we need to be delivered from in our time is pretense, phoniness, blandness, the hypocrisy of the older generation on such matters as sex and race.

The New Morality was more than a mood, however. It was a definite form and style of morality. If its people wished to get rid of conventional norms, they had a norm of their own to replace them: love.

"The New Morality," says Dr. Joseph Fletcher, one of the theologians most associated with this ethic, "separates Christian conduct from rigid creeds and rigid codes. . . . What it does is to treat all rules and principles and 'virtues' . . . as love's servants and subordinates, to be quickly kicked out of the house if they forget their place and try to take over."

> The plain fact is that love is an imperious law unto itself. It will not share its power. It will not share its authority with any other laws, either natural or supernatural.[26]

In practice, this new moral imperative to love was often understood mainly as a way of describing what should characterize purely personal relations. Give any group of college students a few minutes to treat some of the concerns of "the New Morality" and the conversation usually boils down to a quest for guidelines for having sex. But this is not surprising and is certainly not to be condemned out of hand. In the era of the old morality we were so afraid to approach this central subject openly that we created a healthy countervailing interest in the subject among the young.

Too many people, Dr. Fletcher goes on, "like to wallow or cower in the security of the law," the comfort of being told what to do instead of deciding for themselves. "They cannot trust themselves too much to the freedom of grace; they prefer the comfortableness of law. But that, he says, is not love's way. "For real decision-making, freedom is required, an open-ended approach to situations."

In the field of sex morality, for example, Fletcher argues, "we find nothing in the teachings of Jesus ... about birth control, large or small families, childlessness, homosexuality, masturbation, fornication or pre-marital sexual intercourse, sterilization, artificial insemination, abortion, sex play, petting, and courtship." He concludes: "Whether any form of sex (hetero, homo, or auto) is good or evil depends on whether love is fully served."[27] That is why this morality is also called "situation ethics": we proceed by asking not what the law requires, nor by thinking we're free to do anything at all. Rather we ask what, under the circumstances and in the particular situation, *love* requires. (In this respect, we can see a close kinship with part of the justice ethic, which is also situational; but the justice ethic is aimed at public and political dilemmas, whereas "the New Morality" seems to have been employed almost exclusively for guidance in personal encounter situations.)

What went wrong with "the New Morality?"

For my money, we can only welcome a trend toward honesty and openness in people. The impatience of the young is especially welcome when it is turned on the sterile, boring rituals of middle-class society. But there is also another side of it. Hannah Arendt, commenting on the political tragedy that was bound up in the zeal of the French Revolution, remarks that the frenzy for honesty can reach a point at which both the vitals of society and the essentials of being a self are torn away. If we rightly should put down hypocrisy, one still needs the more-than-personal aspects of society, the public forums of law, government, precedent, and history. One needs the protection of having his roles, his own *persona* or mask. The revolutionaries introduced the cult of the "natural man"—but what was left was an erratic society without wisdom which was soon reduced to a military dictatorship; and selves without protection from public clamor, selves who beat a retreat to private life.[28]

A second problem is the undue focus upon the situation in "the New Morality." Most people, young and old, are tempted to consult their own personal situations only, nothing else; they surely do not need to have it urged upon them by a formal ethics to do so. What is needed is advice to keep from defining our situations in an unrealistic but comfortably narrow way. Whether we live in Shaker Heights or Berkeley, we are quickly content with our own illusions, our own "voyage to simplicity." And one of the most attractive voyages of that kind in the years just behind us was the credo of the hippie, that you need only "do your own thing." Says Richard Todd in a study of the recent California hip-world:

Think of all those fresh-faced girls who repeat the *new categorical imperative* with such artless confidence. "I believe anything's moral as long as it doesn't hurt someone else." The ease with which that remark dismisses tradition's offer of advice and asserts its faith in one's ability to weigh the implications of every act—these qualities can find their way beneath the skin.[29]

The temptation to insulate oneself is never far away in the encounter ethic. Its past devotees and exemplars have more than once failed at changing community in America precisely because they withdrew to the fringes of the society, excused themselves on situational grounds, we might say, from having a go at the country's problems. In the case of the recent youth movement, defining the situation all too often meant just dropping out of sight.

What are we to say, finally, of the claimed chief value of "the New Morality," the all-encompassing norm of love?

We have to say, I think, that a value that is used to cover everything covers nothing. If we are to regard love as the only worthwhile value it is not surprising that in practice we find it reduced in discussion and attention to that one area where it can be more or less successfully practiced—the area of purely private relations, especially sex relations.

For people to live together in community requires more than love, and less than love: more, in the sense that a wider list of virtues is needed; less, in the sense that we don't know how, as yet, to do everything lovingly. To concentrate on love as the single greatest virtue, for example, means ignoring the cry of other men for justice, which may go unheeded in the name of a sentimental fixation on love.

Encounter, under the tutelage of "the New Morality," has severe limits. A loving heart cannot be the sole source of politics. Love is possible only when political stability and justice are also possible. To define community purely in terms of a love ethic leads inevitably to privatism, to the very kind of private preoccupation with sex or television or one's personal problems that in fact denies community.

As late as 1970, the youth generation, with its incipient revolution in morality, was still being hailed. Charles Reich wrote a notable book, *The Greening of America*, which partook of this celebration. Now, as we look back over the past few years, Fred Hechinger says, "it is evident that Professor Reich's euphoric account was actually written not at the beginning but at the tail end of a mini-revolution that would not survive the dawn of the new decade."

Asking himself what happened "to the Greening of

America and the Children's Crusade"? Hechinger provides us with a crucial criticism.

The youth culture, he believes, committed a fundamental error by overemphasizing its differences, moral and cultural, from the rest of us. The generations are actually very much alike, once we get past "superficial and overreported" areas of disparity. The potentates of the youth movement, for example, turned out to be "infected by the same viruses that made the older generations so vulnerable and corrupt." Young radicals "quickly succumbed to the same mindless fascination with slogans that had allowed the culture of their elders to become dominated by Madison Avenue values."

Too often, the youth culture had tried to gain community simply by projecting emotions and consciousness. But the future, as Hechinger puts it, requires "shaping" as well as "discovery." America will not be renewed by a movement so unprepared for fundamentals. Quoting a fast line from John Lennon, the one-time Beatles star—"We gotta get down to so-called reality"—Hechinger calls for a more substantial joint effort.

I don't condescend to the young when I believe that we cannot expect them to save the world through some Youth Culture magic. Our culture and theirs are inextricably interwoven, and the Youth Cult's denial of that inescapable truth led to the ultimate collapse of the movement in the '60's and to the present unwarranted retreat into apathy and conservatism.[30]

One of the necessary ingredients of a genuine encounter ethic, let us recall, is a deeper-something, on the order of a "vision," that gives meaning to the encounter experience itself. It is a classic mistake to think that when like-minded people "get in touch with each other," whether via their heads, their bodies, what they smoke, or what music they listen to, community has arrived.

The encounter ethic cannot succeed without a common cause to underwrite the common cup. It must have a tenacious dream of "a new heaven and a new earth." As the most promising locus of the encounter ethic in recent times, the youth movement spoke often about its vision, but was it really a vision? Too often it turned out to be a question of getting away, or tripping, or dividing the house between unregenerate elders and the happy few. As with the other ethics-clusters gone awry, the end result was to diminish rather than build community.

PRELUDE TO REBIRTH?

Buried within us, under the debris of shattered hopes and shredded dreams, is there a more genuine America? So trenchant a critic of the new America wasteland as Theodore Roszak thinks there may be. To be sure, he paints a dark picture:

So a culture works out its peculiar destiny, achieving style, if often at the expense of wholeness. Until, at last, it may lose touch entirely with dimensions of reality which initially inspired its distinctive identity. Then what a people call true will no longer be true as it was once experienced to be true. It will be the mere surface of the primordial experience. . . .[31]

But Roszak goes on to propose the possibility of digging beneath this dead overlay. "It is time to excavate our inherited identity to find there the buried lineaments of the whole personality."[31] Are we about to witness a rebirth of America into a more appropriate, less one-sided identity? I have been saying that I believe so. It cannot be counted a certainty. As the epic of Gilgamesh should remind us, not every initiation experience necessarily succeeds.

Our plight is deeper than a simple failure to live together happily. If that were all, we could hire therapists and be back in business tomorrow morning. Community in America has sunk into death throes because its "warming fires" have been going out. The ethic of the right will, in which community flows as a stream from a fountain, has degenerated into self-righteousness, religiosity, and superpatriotism. The ethic of the rights of man, in which the torch of opportunity is passed from one generation to the next, has been eclipsed by an opportunism that will have success at any moral cost. The encounter ethic, in which people are bound together not only in intimacy, but also in common cause, has yielded to a congeries of travesties, from stroke-me-partner to leave-me-alone-Amerika.

Is there any way out? I believe that there is, and that we have just taken the first step: reckoning with our plight. If we can now see how far we have traveled along the route of Gilgamesh—how wooden, superficial, and self-serving we have let our values become—there is a new chance. After this hard-headed inventory of our ethical resources, stripped of illusions, divested of the temptation to expediency, we may now be ready to take up a new life on the other side of the river. There, paradoxically, what might be lost is offered us again.

V

Ethics As Initiation And Initiative

Hop O' My Thumb (the French *Petit Poucet,* paralleled by the English Tom Thumb) can be seen as far more than an amusing fairy tale. Indeed, once one keeps in mind what some initiation rites are all about—the ordeal of changing from a child to an adult—this old story out of Mother Goose comes to new life.

A poor woodcutter convinces his wife they should take their starving children into the forest and abandon them. The first time they try it, the seven children return safely home, because Hop O' My Thumb, the youngest and smallest, has with alertness dropped pebbles to mark the route.

The woodcutter tries it again. This time Hop O' My Thumb uses bread crumbs, but the birds of the forest eat them. The seven children are lost in the forest. After wandering about terrified, they come to the home of an ogre. The ogre's wife takes them in, tries to protect them from the ogre, who wishes to eat them. Again, the wit of Hop O' My Thumb saves the seven. He outthinks the ogre, who blunders into slicing the throats of his seven ogress daughters, while the seven lads escape.

The ogre pursues them in his seven-league boots. But he pauses for a nap. Hop O' My Thumb relieves the snoring ogre of his boots, puts them on himself, sends his brothers safely home bearing a tidy share of the ogre's fortune. Keeping the boots, which have magically shrunk to fit him, Hop O' My Thumb makes a career for himself as a speedy court courier. He was able to get good jobs for his brothers and bring prosperity to his poor parents.

This story is brimming with initiation motifs. The children are rudely separated from home and mother (in the tale the mother at first protests the abandonment). When the children return home the first time, via the trail of pebbles, we may view this as a case of failed initiation. For they are not changed, nor is the family situation. But the next time, separation truly takes effect, and the ordeals of transition begin.

Of great significance is the locale. Just as the Australian adolescents we looked at earlier were taken by the elders from the settlement to a wooded hill, so the seven children are taken to the forest. For Gilgamesh the zone of transition was a dread river. In other initiation accounts the initiate is swallowed by an animal.

In the European stories, however, the sacred place is the dark forest. It is not inhabited by human beings, nor is it supposed to be, as Saintyves remarks in his fascinating interpretation of Hop O' My Thumb, since initiation is to be conferred "far from prying eyes, . . . in this [place] where one learns all that he needs to know to become a man." The initiators, the "medicine men," the sponsors of the ordeals, are there, of course. These show up in the European stories as animals, giants, ogres, witches, and sorcerers.[1]

Several motifs from Hop O' My Thumb will help us to

see the relevance of initiation themes for understanding our own situation.

1. The initiate at first resists. The Australian boys, we may recall, were frightened at being torn from their mothers. Hop O' My Thumb and his brothers did their best to try to return home. When they realize they are lost in the forest, they are so afraid that they are willing to take refuge in the house of an ogre.

2. Once faced with his ordeal, the true initiate goes on to acquire a characteristic maturity and competence that we will describe later as the ethical quality of *initiative*. Hop O' My Thumb was physically a puny fellow. But his size was no bar to his rising to the occasion. "To merit becoming an initiate," says Saintyves, "to become a man truly worthy of being taken in by the real men of the community, one must first of all show himself to possess sense and intelligence." These qualities are far more important than physical strength or main force.[2]

By now it will be clear that other European fairy tales—such as Hansel and Gretal—may be understood in the same way. Indeed, perhaps the story of Hansel and Gretal makes another crucial point for the contemporary meaning of initiation: it is the young of both sexes, not just the males, who are abandoned in the forest, subjected to ordeals, and challenged to develop maturity.

3. The initiate uses his new maturity not for self-serving ends, but for the good of his fellows, and by extension, of the whole community. Gilgamesh got nowhere, let us recall, because he wanted immortality for himself in a selfish fashion. Hop O' My Thumb, on the other hand, uses his newly discovered gifts to rescue his six brothers. In the primitive sense, the initiate could thus be described as submissive to the tribe, but we shall not go wrong in interpreting contemporary initiation as encouraging bold action for the sake of the community.

4. The initiate takes over power from those who ini-

tiate him and puts it to new, creative use. Hop O' My Thumb becomes the new wearer of the magical boots. He uses them now for better ends. Remarkably, they remain seven-league boots, but they change to fit him.

5. What is at stake in initiation rites are spiritual and educational values. Saintyves helps us to see this point by reflecting on the theme of starvation that sets the whole story of Hop O' My Thumb going. The deprivation of the woodcutter's family is perhaps better seen as allegorical, he says. When it is time for children to become adults, their parents can no longer provide them with sufficient spiritual and educational nourishment, and must send them away for their own good.[3]

INITIATION, THEN AND NOW

As a teacher of ethics in present-day America, I am reminded every day how much my role is like that of the woodcutter. Some kind of ethical famine, as we have seen, has settled in among Americans. We reviewed part of the evidence in our "hard-headed inventory," where we found an impoverished cupboard. The signs are abroad also in a more popular sense. They include a sense of bewilderment, declining faith in historic recipes for living, shaken confidence in institutions. What is in short supply, I think, is the "large, evident option," a sure moral path to follow. Instead, there are seemingly a jillion possibilities, and no such voice of confidence pointing to any of them. Perhaps this vacuum represents a failure of nerve on the part of the elders of the society more than anything else. As a result the young are too surprised, annoyed, and scared—as if they had been abandoned in some black forest of the computer age.

"We're simply pelted by too many choices," was the protest of Sara, a bright psychology major. "Living between the times, when the old ethic is dead and the new one hasn't emerged, is not only frustrating; it's scary." She ended with a plea that universities find a way, without being heavy-handed about it, to help the young today by "coaching them in values."

Maybe she has a point. But we can't keep the children at home. That would be to starve them. They must be put out, once of age, to face the ordeal. If we are to coach them in values, that will have to be done in the forest, or across the river. Gilgamesh, let us recall, does get coaching and help—of a sort. A divine barmaid tells him where to find the ferryman. Reluctantly, the ferryman agrees to take him across. But neither the barmaid nor the ferryman is in possession of saving knowledge: this lies across the river.

The "death throes" of community that we have already talked about are our own contemporary version of the dark forest or the River Styx. We are facing the ordeal now. The bewilderment of Sara, my ethics student, was one micro-part of this ordeal. All those who lived in a moral interregnum, not just the young, may be seen to be crossing over, undergoing initiation; and between the shores we may temporarily lose sight of land.

What shall we find on the other side? Two things, I believe. First, we shall find our roots as a people reexposed, our hopes offered us anew. The knowledge of "where we came from" is a gift like the marvelous plant in the Gilgamesh story, a key to the "secret of life". This rediscovery of roots and hopes is the heart of the rite of *initiation*.

But an offer has to be taken up and a gift used. Thus there is a second aspect, a further test of ourselves.

What will we make of these roots when they are offered us again? How will we refashion the old values to serve new times and coming generations?

To shape an ethic, to relight a warming fire, a response is required to the gift of initiation. I have called the response *initiative*. I have spoken of the full process of ethics as the interplay between *intiation* and *initiative*. Some, I know, will object to the whole notion of initiation as a way of interpreting America's present difficulties in realizing community. Sybil, another student in the same ethics course as the bewildered Sara, expressed her skepticism this way:

"Look, this country's in bad shape," she argued, volubly. "The polls show it. People don't trust the leaders or the institutions. They're falling back on themselves. So how can you be sure we're going to salvage anything out of this mess?"

I tried to answer her. "Community looks dead because it's dying. You're right." Nobody was denying that. "But as it dies to an old form, as we die maybe a little with it, a new chance opens up."

Frank, a quiet pre-med student who sometimes thought maybe he should go live for a while by a mountain lake in the Northwest, answered her.

"People are saying, 'Leave me alone' right now because the country for a long time has had nothing to offer them. We've been invited to wars and fighting and lies and crimes, all in the name of the country. If enough people say 'Leave me alone,' then the market value of wars and fighting and lies and crimes goes down to zero, and we can then have a chance to get together on some better basis."

Thus for Frank, the turning away of the people from "community gone wrong" may itself be a part of the change, part of the turn back to something new and positive.

I had to add that it seemed to me we were already at this turning point. If Sybil's skepticism had a rightly crosshaired target, it was this: What we must continue to be wary of is the outcome. Gilgamesh, after all, made it across the river, learned the secret of life from the wise old couple, and actually had the marvelous plant of life in his hands—only to lose it at the last instant.

As for me, however, what I'm sure of is the chance, the offer. What we make of the offer is something else. But the offer is real.

There are those who complain that the mythology of initiation is not an appropriate way for Americans to understand their heritage. Better to turn to either Christianity or politics. I think we should use the language of myth because it is universal, because its writ runs in these United States just as it did among the Sumerians, the Toltecs, and the Polynesians. The special category of initiation helps us see a dimension of reality lost to those of single vision: that death and rebirth are inextricably tied together. Reality has a "returnability" about it that is not captured in our neat, western, linear view of history. If we dig down into the inner meaning of the more popular lexicons—like those of Christianity and of American politics—we will discover there, too, the language of perennial rebirth. But it may take fresh symbols—the mythology of initiation and initiative—to flush it out, so overlain is it by the layers of clichés and dogma.

Western religion is well stocked with affirmations of the rebirth theme. The notion of the steadiness of God's care, for example, evokes images of a Providence that comes again and again, taking us and the world through crisis to new promise. Even more evocative is the notion of resurrection, described by Kenneth Vaux as "the most persistent eschatological symbol in human history." It is a symbol that comes to the fore typically in times of trouble like ours, says Vaux. In good times it may become quiescent, but it persists.

For the Jew it is witnessed in the persistent Phoenix-like regeneration of a people from the ashes. It is sustained by the faithfulness of God who leads his people out. Among Christians it is sustained by resurrection faith in a Man, who despite D. H. Lawrence's warning, is not "a past number." In Jesus Christ, Man humiliates death. Through his divine operation, lively hope is born even in the midst of tragic history.[4]

Vaux, a specialist in medical ethics, believes in the rebirth of community but does not choose to express it in the language of initiation. Instead, he puts it in theological language. My only argument with him is that this theological framework has now become too particularistic. Vaux can be convincing to me, but that is partly true because we were both theologically trained as neo-Reformationists. He will not be heard by some of my students—young biochemists and civil engineers, candidates for initiation, thorough moderns who learned to trust empirics and sense data as the ancients trusted oracles and seers. Getting them to look beyond the facts is not the problem (as it may be yet for some of their graying science teachers): they are thirsty for the spiritual and the moral. Some are vulnerable to every new religious outfit that comes along—from a pudgy boy guru to the most retrograde version of reductionist fundamentalism. The problem is to get them to see, or see again, their roots and their hopes *on their own,* (like Hop O' My Thumb, taking over the seven-league boots), not through preformed rhetoric. The language of Luther and Calvin, infinitely to be preferred, as far as I am concerned, to the language of the latest guru, or to that of the latest cell of Jesus people, is for all that too caught in the toils of a certain sector of our past to offer much hope as a new binder or new ingredient of a warming fire.

The idea of rebirth could be expressed in *political* language. The American heritage itself offers repeated examples of dark days followed by a new outlook. The death/rebirth theme was expressed best of all by a man who led us in one of the country's darkest moments.

Four score and seven years ago our fathers brought forth on this continent, a new nation, conceived in liberty, and dedicated to the proposition that all men are created equal. . . . we here highly resolve that these dead shall not have died in vain—that this nation, under God, shall have a new birth of freedom—and that government of the people, by the people, and for the people shall not perish from the earth.[5]

But the language of politics and patriotism, like the language of religion, has suffered from heavy misuse and from misplaced narrowness. I have already reported what some students say about America. But even among the good, gray regulars of the society, there is a serious contraction of the notion of what it means to be an American. Patriotism has become another weapon of riot control, to be used against dissenters. It follows that its vocabulary can no longer be a sure way of expressing what we have in common.

We cannot avoid religious and political language. America's concepts of birth and rebirth, of roots and hopes, draw heavily on the resources of politics and religion. But for now—not the old politics and religion. The problem has been well summarized by Theodore Roszak:

If there is to be a next politics, it will be a religious politics. Not the religion of the churches—God help us! . . . but religion in the oldest most universal sense: which is vision born of transcendent knowledge.[6]

The task is to renew the languages of religion and politics so that they can be used again for talking about the American myth. I believe we are at that point: that we are, to use Roszak's figure, in the situation of a journeyer returning: "Ishmael's return from the demonic voyage. . . . A *wise* return, which brings back the full experience of the outward journey."

By now, I think we can see the process of ethics as a dialectic between initiation and initiative. The first is the shock, but also the gift, of a new exposure to our roots and a reaffirmation of our hopes; it reopens both past and future. The second raises the crucial question of our response to this new offer: what happens next depends on the initiative we take.

FROM SOCRATES TO OUTER SPACE

Let's take a closer look at each of these two components of ethics. First, ethics comes on as initiation. It does involve handed-down knowledge, old values. Consider, for example, the moral dilemmas posed by developments like space travel and the new medical technologies. How do we arrive at an "ethics for the space age?" How do we handle the moral questions raised by new life-prolonging medical technologies?

After listening to a room full of space scientists, space historians, and space theologians one day (including a real astronaut), I came to these conclusions:[7]

1. Any development as novel and portentous as the exploration of space promises to shatter old moral patterns and requires their reassembly into a new ethics.

2. There is, so far, a blank spot on the chart: we have no space ethics.

3. Space ethics cannot be the same thing as terrestrial ethics, the kind we had before we could look back at our

own little blue sphere from a spot out there on the way to wherever it is we're going. The experience of man in space cannot be gauged by present political ethics, theological ethics, social ethics, or philosophical ethics.

But no one at this conference really knew what space ethics would look like. It seemed to fall somewhere between medical ethics and ecology. After a day of talking around the subject, space ethics remained almost as empty as space itself. Everyone there intuited, dug the "spiritual" significance of the Apollo flights to the moon. Space religion, space theology, space mysticism, space metaphysics all came easy. There was a pneumatic affinity for space in general—but no clarity about ethics.

Spiritology is a folk phenomenon open to all, but expertise in ethical thinking is not so easily gained. Spiritual exaltation about a new giant step for man is not an adequate basis for a new ethic. Nor can ethical principles be found hiding in scientific data. We cannot even assume that we will always learn, morally, by doing. Traveling beyond the moon will not automatically disclose the fitting values for that venture.

Having a routine medical education, for example, does not in itself qualify an M.D. to handle questions of medical ethics; nor does his happening to be a human being with humanitarian or spiritual impulses qualify him. The first of these parameters, the medical school, may make him into a competent surgeon. The second, his character, may show him to be a moral man who cares about life, love, and justice.

But ethics, as initiation, calls for something more. Ethics is cumulative reflection upon moral values. Ethics is the prism of our identity. It is the process by which we remind ourselves of where we came from, what we stood for, as well as where we are going. Ethics is the renewal of ongoing moral patterns, as well as the quest for emergent ones. We can never cease attempting to

rediscover our roots or looking ahead to our destiny.
Ethics, as initiation, is our principal means of doing so.
And there are definite bodies of knowledge—one of
them running from Socrates to Sartre, another from St.
Augustine to, say, Albert Schweitzer—that provide ac-
cess to this reflective undertaking.

Thus medical ethics, despite the proliferation of new
machines and devices to keep the dying alive indefi-
nitely, is not something wholly new and radically different from earlier ethics. It is, in a powerful sense, the
same old thing—reflection on morality—applied intensively to a particular set of human boundary situations.
It does indeed fix upon new circumstances—modern
medicine and its awesome technology. But its foci are
the perennial dilemmas—about life and death (abortion, euthanasia), love (care for the sick and injured),
justice (who gets put on the dialyzer), and truth
(whether to tell a man he is dying).

Similarly, there will be no space ethics fetched from
scratch out of space science, spiritual appreciation of the
Milky Way, or excitement about the possibility of life on
other planets. We are going to have to have a new ethics,
of course, a space ethics. A future colony of men and
women on the moon, for example, would face a drastically new political and environmental boundary situation, and it would certainly be a fearsome crucible for
moral change. In the meantime, given what we now
know about man, a more practical approach might be to
begin, say, with the subject of morality and morale
among submarine crews, or among the interns in a con-
centration camp, or among the members of the Donner
party—whilst we take a look once again, for collateral
reading, at *The Republic* of Plato, Montesquieu's parable
of the troglodytes, and Governor Bradford's *History of
Plimoth Plantation*.

As we probe further into the universe, new values will

emerge, some old ones will be enhanced, and still others will diminish or disappear. No matter how many galaxies we finally span, it will take ethical thinking—and openness to past values—to keep us human.

Still, there is another side to ethics. Past values untransformed by initiative in the new situation are likely to be dubious values.

A PAUSE AND A LEAP

Jill was a tomboy, a bit overweight, and always fighting with her brothers. She was also intelligent and, as Erik Erickson remembers her before her puberty, there was something about her "which seemed to promise that things would turn out all right."

Erickson goes on to give an account of Jill's coming of age—of a pause and a leap forward, of her coming into an initiative of her own that surpassed the sum of the parts of her initiation into adulthood.

Jill went out West one summer to stay on a ranch. When fall came, she did not go back to college. Instead she got her parent's permission to remain on the ranch. She spent the winter working with horses. She became especially interested in the newborn colts, and soon began to surprise the cowboys with her willingness to get up on the coldest nights to bottle feed the dependent young animals.

Here, on the ranch, far from school and parents, she had learned a vital lesson about life and about herself. She returned home after a while and things, indeed, did "turn out all right." Jill became, Erickson reports, an attractive, mature young woman and a leader.

"I felt that she had found and hung on to an opportunity to do actively and for others what she had always yearned to have done for her," he reflects. Where once

she had shown her needs by overeating, now she handled them, gained control over them, by feeding new-
born colts. By turning what was "passive" into something "active," says Erickson, Jill also "turned a former
symptom into a social act."[8]

We could hardly ask for a better descripton of the
sense of initiative that goes with genuine coming of age,
with true rites of passage.

Young people ready to enter adulthood often bide
their time, Erickson suggests. They pause before they
leap. They are about to bring new energies to bear—not
just physical growth, but also genital maturation, and
new powers of "comprehension and cognition." Above
all, they need a worthwhile cause into which to channel
these energies and throw themselves. Thus they go on a
"search for something and somebody to be true to."
Before taking the leap of fidelity, they may seek a
"moratorium, a period of delay in which to test the
rock-bottom of some truth before committing the powers of body and mind to a segment of the existing (or a
coming) order."[9]

Out of this delay, which corresponds to the transition
or testing period of initiation, comes a new person. The
man or woman who comes to the fore now is a self-
starter; and yet he finds himself only by dedicating his
new energies and gifts to a larger cause than himself.

Even though re-incorporation into the community is
thus the outcome of a genuine initiation experience, we
can no longer think of this outcome in the primitive
sense. For us, the goal of initiation, and the quality of
incorporation back into the community, must be that
change "from a dependent or self-seeking egotist to a
mature man [or woman] with an individual capacity to
judge what should belong to group adaptation and what
should belong to [oneself] alone."[10] It is the quality of
initiative.

So far I have been speaking of initiative as it comes to young persons undergoing initiation. But the same quality is to be expected, no less, of the community itself. When we truly initiate our young, we can expect not only that they will return to the larger company with new powers of initiative. We can and should expect also that the community itself, in its ongoing life, will evince new gifts of initiative.

If I argued in the last section of this chapter that ethics always means looking to the heritage of values, here I have to say just as well that it also means looking ahead to change and to larger things.

This point is well made by John Pfeiffer in his account of the evolution of man.

"In many ways," he argues, "modern men are still a small-band species with a small-band mentality, still creatures wandering in close-knit groups. . . ." It has been easy, since prehominid days, to cleave to family and those physically closest to us. What is hard is "to love more widely and care about anyone outside one's immediate circle and to trust people who look different." What is easy is "to be aroused to quick anger and a fight," even when that is against one's interests. What is hard is "to become aroused about a project involving a community or several communities."[11]

In this sense ethics is at the cutting edge of evolution. The steps we take away from tribehood are not now so much technological steps, despite the marvels of our technology. The big brains that enable us to fashion computers and spacecraft were essentially developed on the primitive savannahs as man became the world's most awesomely successful carnivore. The really intriguing and novel steps now to be taken are ethical steps, as we test whether we can use this same big brain—and, let us hope, this large heart—to think of others and of the future of man.

TRAINEES OF DEAR ABBY

Why is it, a friend asks me, that our public institutions, especially the schools of America, commonly fail at initiation? The reason, I think, is now fairly clear. The schools in this country—and the churches, too, we might add—do not really initiate, if by that we mean "separating the young," putting them to "tests," and allowing them to rejoin us as men and women of initiative. What we do in this country, instead, is to attempt to channel our young directly—a break is regarded as bad form, even though it happens all the time—into the society by means of a restricted set of models geared mostly to production.

Under the circumstances it is not surprising that from time to time the young withdraw, go off on side trips, breaks, and rebellions. They are driven by our inertia to attempt to initiate themselves. The ethics that underwrites community can be found again only when we are ready to let our young arrive at a consciousness of themselves as moral agents setting out in quest of old and new values, and of redefining our hopes. This means growing from being sheltered to being able to decide one's own course of action, in collaboration with his fellows.

Despite past failures to initiate, I have the conviction that a new and better era is at hand, not just for the young, but for the American community at large. We ought to visualize ourselves as a young community undergoing the transition to a new maturity. What we are after is a new set of "warming fires" for American community. Perhaps we know now how to recognize a warming fire when we see it, by using our twin concepts of initiation and initiative. Where do we look?

Let's pretend to be trainees of "Dear Abby," the personal affairs columnist who has been called "the best moral theologian in America today." A letter comes in, saying: "I've got problems—no one pays any attention to me any more." It is signed: GREAT AMERICAN HERO. Let us see what the problems are, what can be done about them, and what we must say to "Dear Great."

VI

Of Heroes, Old And New

"DON'T YOU FIND it interesting that the Vietnamese war and the space effort more or less coincided? I mean, the troop build-up started in the early Sixties. And that's when the President announced the program to land a man on the moon. We were out of Vietnam by 1973—and the last Apollo astronaut was back from the moon."

Up to that moment, I hadn't even thought about it. The question—from a male social worker—came in an idle moment at a cocktail party.

"You think the two were connected, then," I said.

"Absolutely. Here we were in a war we weren't winning, and a war that wasn't going to give us any heroes. Putting a man on the moon would take care of both problems: we'd have a double knockout victory, over the Soviets and over nature; and we'd have a new string of heroes, beginning with Armstrong and Aldrin."

"But the space push isn't over. What about the skylab program?"

"That's a mopping up operation. The heroes were made on the moon."

"Well, there is another spectacular: the joint American-Soviet space flight."

"Heroes in America come out of winning, not from making friends."

My friend's moon-and-heroes version of the bread-and-circuses theory set me thinking about the fortunes of the great American hero in the last few, troubled years of American life.

We can leave to Norman Mailer, or for another day, the subsidiary debate about whether the astronauts really qualify as heroes. I suppose they do. Except for Neil Armstrong and Buzz Aldrin, however, the names of the others who walked on the moon have gradually been forgotten. And after the success of the first mission, Apollo 11, the whole thing became routine TV-watching, not much more exciting than the baseball game of the week—which is to say not very exciting at all.

As candidates for hero, even Armstrong and Aldrin leave something to be desired. Armstrong becomes a professor in Cincinnati and all but drops from public sight. Aldrin has a bout with emotional problems, enters a hospital for psychiatric treatment, and surfaces again with a book telling about his marital infidelity as well as his mental anguish. Mailer does use the imagery of hero (perhaps condescendingly) in his account of Apollo 11, *Of a Fire on the Moon:* "They are heroes, they are first among their peers, the knights of the silent majority, . . ." More often he recurs to the image of a new priesthood dedicated to a new American religion fueled by "some magnetic human force called Americanism, patriotism, or Waspitude"; enabled by technology; and dedicated to a new mission. The Wasp now came into his essence, which had not been realized in the creation of "Protestantism, capitalism, the corporation, or a bastion against Communism." That was a prologue. Now "the Wasp had emerged from human history in order to take us to the stars." They were not astronauts to unravel the mystery of the moon. They were "priests of a religion not yet defined nor even discovered." Here was their real mission: "They were astronauts to save America."[1]

It probably does not matter whether we think of them as heroes respresenting America, or as priests out to save America. For the classic American hero has always been out to offer a promised land of some kind.

But the classic hero figure in America, even if he did have an epiphany in the astronauts, is having his troubles, like the rest of us.

FAREWELL, COMMODORE

The hero we all knew, and maybe loved, seems in fact to have all but disappeared. Take the films, for example. When Lewis Lapham inquired into the mindset of Hollywood movie makers he lamented, among other things, the suppression of heroic figures. The most successful movies of the preceding summer, taking into account both "box office" and critical acclaim, had to do "with rats, lust, greed, and insects." The older admirable qualities of men and women were gone. "In each instance the evil in question triumphs over the rickety moral defenses of the few characters who even bother to raise tentative questions of conscience. A cockroach can be a hero, and a woman is nearly always a whore."[2]

Another *Harper's* writer, David Denby, reached a matching conclusion a bit later: "American movies are terribly diminished at the moment by the almost total absence of *heroines*." Not only has woman's role atrophied in the films. The knack of making "ordinary heterosexual behavior" interesting seems to have been lost. Romance has just about sunk without a trace. There's sex enough, to be sure, "but movies in which male and female equals meet, fight, fall in love, have an affair, get married or don't get married have just about disappeared."[3] (Whether they ever met as "equals" I doubt, for reasons that will presently become clear.)

What explains this decline of heroic figures in our films? Lapham suggests that heroes are still possible, but that film-makers have chosen, for questionable motives, not to portray them. The recent films, he argues, were crass appeals to the under-thirty share of the market. For commercial reasons they cynically pandered "to the worst suspicions of the adolescent mind." Lapham called for the resuscitation of the hero: "A modest hero, certainly, marred by flaws of character, but a figure who might at least suggest occasional aspirations."

What if the hero Americans have worshiped for the past hundred years is really dead? Perhaps the film-makers are simply reflecting the fact. The absence of the hero is notable in other areas of American life as well. Where is yesterday's great-souled, morally robust professional football player? Shouldered aside by players turned playboys, muckrakers, and businessmen. In the comics, the captain of industry, another incarnation of the hero in America, has for years been reduced to parody (General Bullmoose) or the palpably archaic (Daddy Warbucks). And as for the heroic man of state—the patriotic general from the heartland of America who, having vanquished the Nazis, virtuously presided over the fortunes of his fellow citizens as President for eight years—his memory has been obliterated by the spectacle of another President resigning under threat of impeachment for obstruction of justice and abuse of power. Not to mention a Vice President convicted of a felony.

No one is more keenly aware of this decline than the American citizen. "Perhaps at a few other times in history have the American people so craved moral and spiritual leadership," says George Gallup Jr. "The typical citizen is searching for new heroes—but heroes with character, not charisma."[4]

In my opinion it is not the hero in America who has died. It is his recent role. The heroic identity is undergoing massive changes, quite in accord with the cycle of initiation and initiative, death and rebirth, that we have already talked about.

Heroes "die" for very good reasons. They are essentially one-sided figures. They exist to lead the people through a period of crisis or transition. Then they fade, yield.

For three or four generations now the American hero has been aggressive, masculine, and egoistic—a nearly cosmic gladiator figure. He conquers something, or all. ("Winning isn't everything; it's the only thing.") His foes run the gamut from nature to the business world to Hitler to the other football team to space itself. America needed that kind of hero to realize its identity as a great industrial nation and world political force.

But no one is more out of date than yesterday's hero, especially in a new crisis. America's need today is not to establish technological or political hegemony. Even the dread "energy crisis" of the 1970's is not that much of a setback. America has already stormed the technical heights and will soon find a way to refuel its splendid machines. Our true crisis lies elsewhere and is much more serious. As I have been arguing in these pages, our crisis is one of living together—of interdependence. It is a crisis of the cities, of the ethnic groups, of the new nations, of coexistence with other nations. It is a crisis, at every level, of the loss or failure of older structures of community, and of our lack of fresh ones.

Even the astronauts, if one assesses them in Mailer's terms as the spearheads of technological Waspitude, suddenly look more like the representatives of the old era than the archetypes of a new one.

But any view that the classic hero is dying off, it can be argued, is wishful thinking. That is the position of Bernard Murchland, a professor of philosophy at Ohio Wesleyan University. He insists that the gladiator theme is still very much represented in the movies. What about the Godfather? What about Detective Doyle in *The French Connection*? Such figures are very much "aggressive, masculine and egoistic."

Mr. Murchland has a point. The classic hero, the aggressor type, is sticking around. The movie page in my morning paper for Christmas Day, 1973, for example, carried three large ads showing men with guns. One of the films is about "The dirty-tricks squad that even regular cops are afraid of." The question is not the prevalence of such aggressive imagery but whether it meets the real needs of the present. It may be only a kind of rote repetition of symbols, rhetoric, and imprecations that seemed tribally sanctioned in the past.

When Admiral Thomas Moorer, Chairman of the U.S. Joint Chiefs of Staff, was interviewed by Elizabeth Drew, she asked the Admiral: "What about the will of the American people to go out and win wars?"

The Admiral answers that our will is flagging, in his opinion, especially among the young. "It's mandatory for countries such as ours, that has all the blessings and all of the resources and all of the know-how, to move forward and compete and be number one."

Drew: "Number one, militarily?"

Admiral: "Number one in every area, number one in

sports, number one in industry, number one militarily, number one across the board."[5]

Our letters-to-the-editor columns continue to be a national showcase for the old rhetoric of aggressiveness. One reader of *Time* suggested the United States should respond to the Arabian oil embargo in the way anyone should respond to blackmail: "It is not just a matter of oil, it is not just a matter of economics, . . . It is a question of national integrity and honor, or are these dead?"[6] The mayor of Macon, Georgia, a law-and-order man, said he wanted to go to Congress, and that if he won, he'd offer a job to Lt. William Calley, convicted of murdering Vietnamese civilians.[7] Readers of the *States-Item* in New Orleans were writing letters praising the police superintendent for ordering his men "to get their hair cut and sideburns and mustaches trimmed" so as to move "Back to 'the masculine look.' "[8]

In many situations, of course, the old virtues are much more than nostalgic talk. They still serve a useful function, if not to surmount a new crisis, at least to get some of the world's work done. Ross Perot, the phenomenally successful Texas businessman, having taken over a major Wall Street investment firm, set about recruiting executives from among "outstanding ex-military officers." His recruitment message is almost a summary, in non-pejorative terms, of the attributes of the classic American hero figure. "We have found the military officer has learned to work effectively under pressure," said Perot, "to make good decisions quickly, and to lead and motivate others in getting the job done.

We need people who are honest, smart, tough and self-reliant. We need people who have an excellent history of past performance, big personal goals for the future, and a willingness, through service and hard work, to make these goals materialize.[9]

Who would disparage these qualities? Who can fault the firm that wants men who are willing to work hard? Not I, certainly. I am an ex-naval officer myself. Ambition and industriousness are virtues I admire. I also like feminine women, follow college football and go out to win when I play tennis or racquetball. The classic American heroic virtues are still a part of me, of all of us—in rhetoric here but in substance there; in the mass media, in the movies and other art forms, and in the consciousness of many Americans. Some of these virtues, I have conceded, are even admirable. But I believe that alongside this older image of hero—typically aggressive, masculine, and egoistic—a new heroic figure is appearing in America. And I believe that the new hero, rather than the old one, will have to bear the burden of our contemporary crisis, our new plight, and show us a way through it.

Our struggle must now be to find, or to refind, the roots of community, new "warming fires." The question is whether an older mythical image, the old hero, however useful in other ways, can be truly "saving" for America in its present hour. Whichever image is more "saving," the old or the new, will also evidently be, by that very fact, more "living."

The older hero led us into becoming a great technological force and political power. But our national "salvation need" has now shifted. The older image of hero cannot any longer "save" us from what is a new kind of lostness, the old image suffers the fate of any symbol that no longer truly symbolizes: it is dead or dying. Our new crisis is not one that can be surmounted by Horatio Alger's kind of man. We do not need, this time around, reincarnations of Commodore Vanderbilt or of Theodore Roosevelt or of John Wayne, or even of JFK standing up to the Russians in West Berlin. We need a new hero—and he is emerging.

THREE MARKS OF THE NEW HERO

Roosevelt Grier, former professional football player (New York Giants, Los Angeles Rams), has turned out a book on needlepoint. He happened to be good at this putatively feminine craft, and nothing about his hobby seemed to make him any less a man.

"My buddies used to tease me," Grier reflects, "but as it turned out, I had the last laugh. They are all doing it now and can barely remember the time when they used to rib me."[10]

I escorted a young woman executive to a dinner party one night, and was shaken to discover that she flies a plane. My surprise, however, was only a sign of somnolence about what's happening. That she was a "better man than I" at something I wouldn't dream of undertaking makes her no less a woman.

Signs of change are all about us. The emergent reality of the new American hero may be seen by anyone willing to look. The classic American hero figure, I have said, is overly masculine, egoistic, and aggressive. Let's begin with "Overly Masculine," and see what countersigns are appearing.

Long hair on males represents a return to the sexual and anthropological center; a less harsh, one-sided masculinity is now called for. For some time now, come to think about it, boys and men have been able, without embarrassment or threat to their masculinity, to learn to play the piano and cook and keep house, even to wear what used to be exclusively a female accessory, the purse. The latter, when worn by men, is called, with perhaps a lingering touch of camouflage, an "outside wallet." I have a blue-denim version of the same, complete with shoulder strap. I should say it is the best investment, except for my bicycle, that I have made since moving to Houston. It is identical in construction to a woman's large, ordinary purse. A couple of weeks ago a businessman carrying an attaché case approached me in the bank, and asked where I had bought it.

"Looks much more practical than this thing I have here with no straps," he said. "I want one like yours."

If all this is a softer masculinity, it is also a more balanced representation of the human. The women's liberation movement represents a corresponding trend toward the center. Women are rightly asking for the end of an era in which they were made to serve as maids for gladiators. In an age when concern for lost community will be far more important than gladiating, women are bound to recover roles at the center of the action—and be able to hope, for the first time in American history, to exist as the true equals of men.

Ancient initiation rites and legends, such as the story of the quest for the Grail, are surprisingly even-handed when it comes to gender. "All through the story," says Joseph L. Henderson, a follower of Carl Jung, "we find a more or less symmetrical balance between male and female figures. . . ."[13] Earlier I mentioned the ancient legend of Gilgamesh, and his wandering quest for the secret of life. Now let me repeat two fascinating details. First: Gilgamesh, in finding a way to get across the "waters of death," gets help from two figures: a man and a woman. The woman, a "divine barmaid," gives him directions. The man, a ferryman, takes him across. Second: When Gilgamesh reaches the realm beyond, where he can learn the secret, he finds a man-and-wife team rather than a solitary male figure. The old man, Utnapishtim, consults his wife. "Look at the strong man who wants life everlasting," he says to her. "Sleep like a fog blows upon him." The woman gives her advice: "Touch him that the man may awake. That he may return in peace . . . to his land."[12]

In other words, the secret of life comes from a symbolic union of male and female. "Androgyny" is the technical term for it, drawn from Greek roots meaning literally "man-womanness." An MIT economist, Dr. Mary P. Rowe, thinks the time has come for us to get used to the word and to the idea. "Androgynous people express spiritually both 'masculine' and 'feminine' qualities to the extent that they choose," she says. "They can be gentle and strong, wise and tender, dynamic and passive at times." A great deal of our frustration and unhappiness is linked with what Dr. Rowe calls "polarizations between the sexes and inside us." Such exaggerated and separated sex roles, she suggests, must be diminished in the world to come, replaced by a more balanced image: "We are moving toward each other and toward our other halves." In this change, everyone benefits:

Men on the whole gain options to love. Women stand to gain equal pay for equal work, and enormously wider opportunities for independence and status and creativity.... Androgyny means wider choice of both love and work for both men and women.[13]

I would suggest that a move toward balancing sex roles will do its bit to rekindle the "warming fires" of community. For now we can better see the work of achieving solidarity as a joint venture between the sexes rather than as a tribal print-out exalting males and putting down females. One attribute of the new hero, and of the new community, in America will surely be "androgyny." Let's translate that term into plain English and say simply that in our quest for new heroic traits that can lead us past crisis toward the secret of community, we need not the overpowering men and the passive women of past stereotypes, but men and women who share the burden of caring and doing.

What happens, in the second place, to the "overly egoistic" side of the classic hero figure?

Here, too, signs of change abound. American egoism, extended against other men via politics and the military, and against nature via technology, has reached its limits and is now being replaced by cooperation.

When he visited the United States in 1973, the Chairman of the Soviet Communist Party, Leonid I. Brezhnev, met with fifty-one leading American business officials. These included bankers, industrialists, oilmen, and aircraft exporters. Chairman Brezhnev urged active trade between the two countries.

"It has to happen," said the chairman of Tenneco. "The world has to get together and it will." Tenneco let it be known that it was investigating investment prospects in the Soviet Union.

"Look through history," suggested the chairman of a Texas construction firm, sounding dramatically unlike some of his heroic predecessors. "People of different ideologies have got to do business together. . . . Why should we impose our form of government on them?"[13]

The cynical may argue, of course, that there's nothing really new here, that a rich man will trade with anyone, even his ideological enemy, if he sees a chance of making a buck. Whatever the motives involved national egoism is really receding.

What about egoism as it interferes with lesser levels of community, among individuals and groups? We need to remind ourselves of the varied shapes that egoism has taken in America. It is sometimes a matter of a man, a leader, a tycoon, putting his stamp on everything around him, including people. A recent Democratic president comes to mind, who brought to the White House familiarity with the branding iron, and also a fondness for his own initials. (Yet one does not have to be a "big man," or woman, or even to possess power, to manifest the attitude.)

Perhaps it is a modest sign of hope to recall that the

day of the great American individualists seems over, that our one-man empire builders, our Henry Fords and our John D. Rockefellers, are gone, replaced by team management. But there is a danger here. Individualism has been superseded by corporate egoism —which is even more intractable, according to the theologian Reinhold Niebuhr in his incisive study of the early 1930's, *Moral Man and Immoral Society.* His thesis was "that a sharp distinction must be drawn between the moral and social behavior of individuals and of . . . groups, . . ." Individuals may be conceivably capable of a fair amount of justice, reason, and objectivity even where their own interests are involved. Such achievements, at best more difficult, may flatly be impossible for groups.[14]

As we have just seen, however, in the example of the businessmen consorting with the Communist party chairman, even corporate momentum can shift, swept along into the future by an emerging change of identity. Even our industrial machine can be infected, and changed, by the new currents.

We move closer home, nearer the lives of most of us, when we observe that machines and technical hardware serve marvelously as an extension of the personal ego. As one television commercial for a hand-held calculator has it, "I was a dummy"—until I got myself an X-brand electronic brain. As a confirmed pedestrian, bicycle rider, and jogger, I have observed this transformation hundreds of times on the public streets. I have been forced off the road by women driving Cadillacs, hippies in fifteen-year-old Chevvies, farmers in pickup trucks with populist bumper stickers, and even by a gentle, fragile sophomore student of mine.

Still we are not to the most characteristic American egoism. Car-egoism is at least as common to France or Italy as to the U.S. What we must do is take this egoism of enhancement by technological extension, and see it in a political or patriotic context. That is the worst. And the test question is: do we see signs that this worst of all American egoisms is being ameliorated?

Two of the nations especially hit by the Arabs' political decision in 1973 to curtail oil shipments were the Netherlands and the U.S. It occurred to numerous Americans, but I daresay to few or no Hollanders, to call for military intervention against King Faisal of Saudi Arabia. The difference lay in our having massive technology with which to extend one's personal and patriotic ego.

An Australian clergyman whom I met at a conference in the Texas Medical Center put it bluntly:

"Until you got in trouble in Southeast Asia, you Americans thought you *were* the world. Most of you still do."

"You mean we thought we were *managers* of the world?" I said, thinking that this was bad enough.

"No, the world. Not just its managers. Not even the center of the world. The world itself."

Is this most virulent of egoisms receding? I believe it is. Why did we get out of Vietnam? Frustration and failure had much to do with it, but can't fully explain our withdrawal. We got out of Vietnam for an additional reason: the common-sense realization that America, henceforth, is only part of the world, and a part that has to get along with the other parts.

One other side of our American egoism needs to be recalled: our self-extension upon, over, and at the expense of, *nature*. Again, the technological extension of the self seems to be at the heart of the difficulty. The American hero of the recent past has not only been politically puissant, he also has been idealized as subjugator of the earth, including all of the mountains, valleys, seas, dirt, and rocks, and even potentially the stars. The worst of it is not our aggressiveness (a theme we come to next) or even the tragic effects of it upon nature; but rather the awful divorcement from both fellows and from nature that our egoism has implied, and which amounts to an impossible contradiction: when one defines himself unilaterally, whether against man or nature, that *eo ipso* leaves him naked and vulnerable.

But changes are coming into focus here, too. Indeed, one can sense that a new identity is in course of happening to us. The opposite of ego-extension, whether via technology or politics, is cooperation, or in Ivan Illich's expressive term, "conviviality":

I want it to mean autonomous and creative intercourse among persons, and intercourse of persons with their environment, . . . I consider conviviality individual freedom realized in mutual personal interdependence and, as such, an intrinsic ethical value. I believe that without conviviality life becomes meaningless and persons wither.[15]

Rely less on technology and on political muscle, is the message here. Rely more on commerce with others, commerce of the self seeking another self. Rely more on the natural, which ought to be approached by reunion as much as by domination. Is this new motif of conviviality at work? I believe it is.

In California, of late, a group has been planning a new town in which automobiles would be banned altogether. The aim: to create a community "where people could grow and relate to each other in a warm, experimental atmosphere." The planned town, of 3,000, would substitute walking, bicycling, and horseback riding for automobiles. "The big problem in our nation," said the coordinator, Christopher Canfield, "is a lack of a sense of community. We have a broad cross section of people who are seriously interested—laborers, office workers, professional people, artists, . . . all across the income spectrum."[16]

In Houston we have been treated to a striking example of lessened corporate egoism toward nature. After years of complaints that its coke plant was polluting the ship channel, Armco Steel Corporation decided to switch rather than fight. "The reason we've been linked with pollution seems quite simple," observed a vice president of the firm. "We've been polluting." He recommended that the coke plant be closed, that all employees be offered alternate jobs, and that the firm ship in its coke supplies from non-polluting sources elsewhere.[17]

Egoism, whether personal, corporate, or national, is a form of immaturity. It is often, as we have seen, a kind of defensiveness. "Selfhood" at any of these levels is better served by conviviality—which, in substituting cooperation for ego-extension, gives us a new basis of community. The new hero shows us not how to flex muscles, but how to live together.

After this exploration of egoism and its countertrait, conviviality, we are already bordering on the third issue, that of the aggressiveness of the classic hero figure. Here we move from a *state* of character, egoism, to the kind of *action* that corresponds to the state of character, aggressiveness. All of its qualities are summed up in the title and subtitle of a recent book on guns by Robert Sherrill. Note the verbs:

The Saturday Night Special:

And Other Guns With Which Americans Won the West,
Protected Bootleg Franchises, Slew Wildlife,
Robbed Countless Banks, Shot Husbands Purposely and by Mistake,
& Killed Presidents
Together With the Debate Over Continuing Same

The book itself exposes the continued resort to aggressiveness in American life. But I say a new option is available, one far superior to the old for action in our contemporary crisis. The quality surpassing aggressiveness in our emergent "new hero" is not passivity, as apologists for the hard old virtues might charge. Nor should it be. Aggressiveness—the pursuit of egoistic ends by insensitive, harsh means—is countered by a new pursuit that flows out of conviviality. This new style of action retains all of the qualities of brisk, intrepid "doing." But now it becomes action on behalf of others as well as self, and by means that take care of others, and of nature. What shall we call it? We learned the name of it in the last chapter, when we were talking about rites of passage. It is the quality of *initiative,* action aimed at care for neighbor and nature.

In the annals of American feistiness, head-knocking, and fisticuffs, perhaps no activity better illustrates the folklore of aggressiveness than the trade union strike. Yet union leaders are increasingly questioning the wisdom of using this right. It may be hard for some to believe the day will come when unions rarely strike. Nevertheless, sentiment has been growing among labor leaders that strikes for better-paid workers "just don't make sense."(George Meany).[18]

Evidence comes in that we can do our business in this country without wasting men and the earth. Early in this decade a fire swept the Sunshine Silver Mine at Kellogg, Idaho. Ninety-one men died. Within two years mine workers were calling it the safest mine in their experience. The company added some $3,000,000 in safety improvements. Stricter fire drills and rescue training were begun. Union members experienced a renewed sense of common purpose. Morale went up.

"This has got to be the safest mine around now, no

question about it," said Larry Martin, one of the miners.[19]

In one Southern state, conservation officials were worried about the public reaction to stricter controls over hunting. Cost of a hunting license was increased. Bag limits were better enforced. But the concern was misplaced. Most hunters are reasonable people. They found they could still get the symbolic reward of tramping the wilds with gun in hand if they made one or two, rather than seven or eight, hunting trips during the season. In Georgia, Senator Herman Talmadge went even further. Relaxing from Washington duties at his country farm, Talmadge admitted that he was becoming reluctant to shoot deer.

Another senator, one of well-earned conservative profile, Strom Thurmond, of South Carolina, seemed to have shifted his identity a bit, also. A television news program showed him and a black woman from his state, a civil rights leader, engaging in lavish mutual praise. The woman, referring to some of Thurmond's actions on behalf of blacks, said it was as if he had gotten religion.

These senators may not be the scions of a new ethic. I suspect that they consider themselves to be devotees of the older virtues. But that shows the potency of change: even the identity of the spokesmen for the old begins to shift.

There will be those, even among proponents of a new American ethic, who will argue for the continued role of aggressiveness in human nature. Erich Fromm, critical of the violence in American life, still sees a place for aggression—as a "natural defense" against threats to life. As such, it serves survival. What should be condemned instead, he says, is *destructiveness;* the problem with America is that it has become the world's most destructive society.[20]

The classic hero figure is counterproductive, however, not because he responds to threats—which is natural—but that he is "overly" aggressive; not that he is competitive, but that he, in the words of Walter Rauschenbusch, exalts a combativeness that "pits men against one another in a gladiatorial game in which there is no mercy." Rauschenbusch, whose views anticipated the new values we see emerging today, recounts the bitter jest of an uneasy railroad president in New York: "The men who go down town on the Elevated at seven and eight o'clock really make things. We who go down at nine and ten, only try to take things away from one another."[21]

The new heroic virtue of initiative—action aimed at care for neighbor and nature—far from ignoring threats to survival, seems to me to be aimed exactly at protecting life. I should say, however, that survival—*mere* survival—is far too meager an end. We are "surviving" right now. But without community, survival is a poor consolation. What we must hope for is an ethic that not only permits continued survival, but one that brings us in out of the cold, draws us once again into the redeeming, warming presence of each other.

It is toward this kind of ethic that I believe the emerging "new heroic virtues" point.

CLUES FOR ETHICS AND COMMUNITY

The exaggerated masculinity of the older hero diminishes in favor of a more central affirmation: man and woman in complementarity. (Perhaps that also symbolizes ethnic, racial, and other sorts of mutual acceptance.) The older egoism withers—prompted by facts of life, such as the frustrations of Vietnam and an energy crisis—and a new spirit grows, which we have called "conviviality." The new spirit moves us to find resources in each other rather than in machines as extensions of lonely selves, and to a new alliance with nature and the environment. Aggressiveness, in its destructive form, yields to the energetic sense of moral initiative, which is just as active and intrepid, but which ventures out to care for others and for nature in the hope that we may not merely survive, but that we may recover community.

What will be distinctive about this new ethic, especially when we compare it with the older American ethics clusters?

First, we must now come to grips in a new way with the challenge of *interdependence.* Men have always depended on each other, of course, from the primitive time when our ancestors learned that meat eating and sharing go together, that killing big game meant cooperation, that eating it meant carting it jointly back to a shared camp or home base.

Still, interdependence has been a local option, a limited venture, until modern times. The Puritans truly believed themselves a holy commonwealth, a community of men and women banded together under the Word of God. Yet where sainthood ended, there the lines of interdependence notably began to weaken. Similarly, the warriors for justice in our history have long evinced a sense of social solidarity with the downtrodden and the disinherited. At the same time, the very heart of progress, for the justice-seekers, lay in pursuing a disparageable adversary—the despot on the British throne, the slave-holders, the capitalist exploiters of the working man. As for the communitarians, their sense of interdependence was focused, usually, on those present in living relationships; however kin its members may have deemed themselves with other men, however much a part of the world-soul they may have supposed themselves to be, the action remained concentrated.

Now the claim of interdependence has to be more fully recognized. It becomes central to ethical thinking. It is the fundamental reality that has to be considered in rebuilding community.

There is an easy way and a hard way to tackle an ethic of interdependence. The easy way is the verbal approach: to talk on and on about "one world," our "global village," the wonder of "instant communication," and the miracle of seeing ourselves as "world citizens," renouncing, as it were, background and nationality. Instead, I recommend that we do it the hard way. We must embrace interdependence and look for ways to build ethics upon it. At the same time we must acknowledge that we are who we are, and that we come from where we come from. Owning our pasts and our identities, we must seek to turn our limitations, in an epic rite of passage, into ways of getting on with others in the future.

As I have tried to show by sketching the image of the new hero, we are headed toward this passage. The new balance of male and female; the new sense that it is better to depend more on each other, less on machines; new tendencies away from over-aggressiveness and toward a style of initiative that seeks the good of others —all of these are really ethical guidelines anchored on the reality of interdependence.

Interdependence is one base for new ethical thinking. But there is one other broad ethical category that now has to be rethought. Let me put it this way. Interdependence is the ethical *challenge* of our era. We must think not only in terms of challenges, but of responses to challenge. What ethical symbol may best be commandeered for *answering* to the challenge of interdependence?

None of the favorite "answering symbols" of the ear-

lier ethics clusters will quite do the job. The Puritan
bedrock notion of God's grace still has much to convey,
but it is a silted-over symbol of one religion, and it cannot appeal to some segments of our pluralistic society.
Symbols drawn from the rights-of-man philosophy
speak exultantly to part of our problem; but justice
alone, however essential, does not achieve community.
To justice, as theological ethicists have been saying in
various ways for centuries, must be added some expression of love. From the encounter ethic we can draw the
symbol of love as practiced in close-knit communities;
but this symbol often fails to convey the urgency of public measures needed to enable and permit community.

The best "answering symbol," I believe, is the notion
of *care* and *caring*. It is the one symbol rich and broad
enough to take in the diversity of our contributing traditions. The practicing Jew enters our community with
chesed, God's loving-kindness, in mind. The convinced
Christian thinks of *agape,* God's self-giving love as manifested on the Cross. The secularist weighs in with the
ideal claim of one self on another, summed up in the
symbol of *justice.* All of these currents can be expressed
in the contemporary imperative of caring for the other.

No one, as Martin Buber once commented of a
dialogue among diverse parties, need give up his point
of view. What happens, if community takes place, is that
the several partners "unexpectedly . . . do something
and unexpectedly something happens to them which is
called a covenant." Sticking to their own commitments,
they are also able, in this new coming-together, "to let
themselves run free . . . for an immortal moment."[22]
That is a description of what happens to us when we are
present to one another, when we proffer community,
when we care.

Caring is a compact symbol for the virtues of the new
hero: parity, conviviality, and initiative. Caring is prob-

ably the central ethical ideal of our times, and it leads quite directly to the idea of community:

In the context of a man's life, *caring* has a way of ordering his values and activities around it. When this ordering is comprehensive, because of the inclusiveness of his carings, there is a basic stability to his life; he is "in place" in the world, instead of . . . merely drifting or endlessly seeking his place.[23]

I believe the coming new value orientation in America can best be described as an ethic of interdependence and care. But what is new must arise, phoenixlike, out of what went before. The new heroic qualities that flesh out the ethic of caring were foreshadowed in the older American values. Perhaps we are ready now, combining new insights with old, to strike the flint of a new "warming fire".

VII

To Light A New Fire

ON A DAY in May, 1945, the Swedes learned that the Nazi yoke had been lifted from the shoulders of their neighbors in Denmark and Norway. Anders Nygren, the Swedish theologian, described that day as a time "their hearts broke loose!" "Those who experienced those days, and the sensation of jubilation which gripped all because of that message," he said, "have an illustration of what a message, an overwhelming story of good news, joyful news, really is." They know what gospel means. With that kind of news, "One can breathe again, and begin to love."[1]

Today, I believe, we are being offered good news that is just as momentous and liberating. It is the message that we are henceforth free to care for one another. It is the assurance that caring itself is reason enough for the human enterprise. It is the discovery that nothing else matters as much. It is the promise that caring will go on, indeed flourish, amid the troubles of civilization. For some of us, and I include myself in this number, the ultimate guarantee of the matter is that God cares for us, and that we act out that divine care, make it real, as we care for others.

Let me illustrate the temper of my hopes by reflecting for a moment about a recent piece of scary news, the so-called energy crisis. I believe it signals the kind of good news that I have been talking about.

The movie, *American Graffiti,* is a retrospective film about a night in the life of a group of young people just finishing high school in the spring of 1962. Nearly all of it takes place in automobiles. Carloads of boys and girls cruise the streets, searching for dates and excitement. Two young men with souped-up cars bring it all to a climax near dawn with a drag race on the edge of town. Terry, a bespectacled, hapless fellow, is nearly out of it, since he commands only a Vespa scooter, not even quite a motorcycle. Then Steve, who is supposedly going away the next day to college in the East, turns his car over to Terry for safekeeping. Terry comes to life, joins the cruising bands, and soon has a willing blonde seated alongside him. The evening is tumultuous. Terry leaves the keys in the car. Two toughs steal it. He finds them and the car, but they almost beat him up—until he is rescued by a pal who roars up in his yellow racing job. In the end Steve stays home, takes his car back, and Terry's new girl friend, rather than walk, switches to some other guys with a car.

If the cowboy was the symbol of the great nineteenth-century American dream, the automobile was undoubtedly that of the twentieth—up to here, at least. Perhaps 1962 was a fitting moment to be captured in a film about youth and cars, for within a few years afterward, the car culture had visibly begun to decline in the wake of pollution, congestion, rising costs of gasoline, and a feared world scarcity of fossil fuel.

Within a decade an ecologist was calling for a radical revision of Western morality to take account of the need to conserve energy, since "strong morality apparently has a survival role in programming power budgets." A new "Ten Commandements" would be needed, including this injuction: "Thou shalt not waste potential energy." In this new energy ethic, sin would be defined as "excessive power dissipation." The automobile, far from remaining the symbol of beatitude that it had been for us through the 1960's, would now fall to the despised status of something like the baals, or false gods, of the Hebrew Bible. The love of speed and luxury in automobiles, all too dominant hitherto in our culture, would now come to symbolize gross immorality.[2]

This is all imaginative and helpful and it tells us important things about the way morality had better change in America. Now we had better prefer efficiency over waste, rate stability a little higher, and seek better rapport with nature.

But there is an even more revealing side to the energy crisis; there is positive good news wrapped up in it. It becomes a symbol of our new freedom, so to speak, to put care ahead of cars.

Am I just imagining things? When I walk a block to Kirby Drive, a six-lane spillway between Astroworld and River Oaks, I see it is crowded with cars. They come in great floods. Most of them still exceed the speed limit.

No, I am not imagining things. Kirby Drive is no longer the only game in town. Last night on public television I listened to a panel of young students of car design. They decried a civilization that makes your driver's license your principal I.D. They cast a cold eye over such foibles of our recent past as the cosmetic annual model change, overweight cars, performance features (brakes, suspension) not up to those of smaller European cars.

Americans will still have a romance with the car, one of them said, but now it will be tempered with honesty. It is still in to walk in Europe, I thought, though they have great cars there.

But the car is only an example of a larger point. By depending less on the props of technology we shall certainly be led to depend more on each other. Thus our interdependence is scored anew, and a new emphasis is laid on what was always of first importance: the quest for the "good community" in the inward sense, be it called salvation with the Puritans, happiness with the revolutionaries, or a vision of peace with the encounter groups. Let us return then, to our three primal value clusters—righteousness, justice, and encounter—and see if the news of emerging interdependence and care cannot pry loose the crusted layers, and release dancing new fires of the American spirit.

RIGHTEOUSNESS REVISITED

There is new life and activity on the religious front in America today. Some of this ferment goes one way, some another. All of it shows a hunger for something to fasten onto and to believe in, a dissatisfaction with recent doldrums, and a groping about, sometimes wrong-headed, for good news. An unusual event occurred recently in Houston's Astrodome. On a high platform at one end of the football field, sat twenty-four "mahatmas" or disciples. Still higher, on a blue throne that towered some three hundred feet from the ground, sat a teen-age Indian religious leader, called "perfect master" by his followers—Guru Maharaj Ji. To see and hear him came as many as 15,000 persons a day, most of them alienated young seeking an alternative both to the drug counterculture and to straight society. A reporter asked an associate of the guru's why the movement had caught on. "In America," came the reply, "everyone's stomach is full but people have spiritual needs."

Rennie Davis, a recruit from the fading New Left, called it "the most revolutionary movement that's ever come down the pike; it's a fundamental threat to every institution rooted in ego and pride."[3] What was so marvelous, he told another writer, "is that everyone has the same vision. . . . After the infighting . . . , the quibbling, the disorder, to have the *unity* we were talking about in the Sixties. . . ."[4]

In the very same year a United States senator from Iowa announced his resignation in order to enter religious work. A former aide of the President, a laywer who had been implicated in the Watergate scandals and had the reputation of being a "tough guy," announced his dramatic conversion to evangelical Christianity. He and the senator, separated by political differences, announced a friendship of reconciliation.

A former astronaut described his journey into space, which included orbiting the moon on the Apollo 14 mission, as a religious experience: "My view of our planet, suspended like a tiny blue and white jewel against the immense black velvet sky, was a glimpse of divinity."[5] He turned down high-paying jobs to set up an ecology equipment firm, most of the profits to go to psychic research.

This spiritual milling about, some of it distasteful —certainly to me—points to the end of a cycle, and the beginning of a new one. Older versions of the American dream have proven inadequate, or out of date, or unable to satisfy. But that failure, according to two students of the American experience, "seems now to have opened us to the inner or spiritual dimension of religion." And this means more than a religion of convenience, social concern, or outward national success. It means that our usual ways of looking at and measuring social phenomena may fail to see what is going on: "The crush, the violence, the noise and the harshness of contemporary American life will renew the press for transcendence in ways no strict empiricist could predict or be happy to see."[6]

What this new situation means is that community can once again be visualized as flowing out of inward spiritual impulses. That sounds almost like the first Puritans who, let us recall, thought that divine grace, converting the heart, was a fountain for the nourishment of common life.

We can't go home again. We can't relive the Puritan experience. Indeed, who would want to? Nevertheless, there are some ideas to be salvaged from the older "righteousness ethic" that may help us to strengthen the possibilities for a spiritual renewal in our own time. I see at least these three:

1. In American life, we must be bolder in acknowledging the inward impulse to others, the yearning for the transcendent that is struggling today within us.

2. Inward warmth—the disposition toward caring, as we may call it—has to be embodied in outer structures. For the Puritans the outer was an alliance of church and state. For us it is more likely to be a contest among technology, state, church, and other institutions.

3. Caring for others, as a new American ethic, has three dimensions—remembering our roots, anticipating the future, and experiencing the present. The Puritan heritage has much to say, in particular, about remembering our roots.

Let us take up these themes one at a time.

First, let us see how new interest in the inner side of man may help us overcome a one-sided picture, the picture of man as a being who may be measured, whose behavior may be predicted, whose destiny, so to say, may be computerized.

In East Lansing, Michigan, a social scientist, Dr. Harold J. Spaeth, has been using the Michigan State University computer in a fascinating new pursuit: predicting the outcome of cases argued before the U.S. Supreme Court. Over a three-year period he successfully forecasted about eighty-five percent of the decisions.

Among the cases he missed were those involving capital punishment and abortion. "The odds the court would find abortion laws unconstitutional were about 9 or 10 to 1," said Dr. Spaeth. Why did the Court rule the other way? He wasn't sure. Perhaps, he speculated, the Court "found a new right, the right of privacy."[7] Perhaps, we might speculate, these areas—dealing as they do with the giving of life and the taking of life —take us into the most unfathomable reaches of the human condition.

Spaeth's work is in the best tradition of American social science. Quantification and prediction is still the name of the game. "Even the best-informed guesses are not good enough," the sociologist William F. Ogburn insisted. "We must measure, and measure precisely."[8]

What is it that social scientists measure? It may be clear enough what the physicist measures—I have a feeling it is less and less clear even there—but what is it, in the realm of man and his groups, that is to be examined with such precision? The French sociologist Raymond Aron has pointed to a kind of hidden uncertainty that haunts all such endeavors in his field. As a scientific discipline, sociology rightly seeks objective knowledge. Yet it is presented with a frustratingly elusive target: "What it claims to know objectively and scientifically is some vaguely defined thing we call society." The content and meaning of this object of measurement varies

so much from one country to another that Aron
thought the definition of sociology itself could hardly be
fixed: "I prefer to regard as sociology that which
societies designate as such."[9] Thus American, Marxist,
and French sociologists will have their own ideas about
what it is they are studying, and how they should go
about it.

It is not that we must not try. But precision may be an
overemphasized attribute in the study of man and his
communities, especially if it is purchased at the expense
of reflection on what it is that we seek to examine: man
himself and his hopes.

There is a new openness showing itself today. There
is new recognition that we can't understand ourselves
without thinking about spiritual values and moral con-
victions.

Erich Fromm comes to a like conclusion. America's
industrial expansion has been accompanied by growing
insensitivity, he said. We are so numbed by goods and
machines that we routinely accept violence.

"The United States is not yet entirely in hell," Fromm
commented. "There is a very small chance of avoiding
it, but I am not an optimist." Where does that chance
lie? In the hope that Americans will no longer buy material expansion "at a sacrifice of, what shall I call it, the
soul." The chance lies in recourse to the "religious and
humane tradition" in America, "in which the proper
goal of society is to serve its members." What is urgent
now "is a renewal of a sense of general religious
values."[10]

A giant step was taken by the French paleontologist
and theologian, Teilhard de Chardin, with his insistence
that reflection about human beings has to include "the
within" as well as "the without". That is the only way, he
thought, that we can understand what is truly significant about human evolution. If we are "to give man his

natural position in the world of experience, it is necessary and sufficient to consider the *within* as well as the
without of things." Seeing only the without misses the
significance of thought, the psychic, the affinity of one
thing for another. This external mode of viewing finally
"breaks down completely with man, in whom the existence of a within can no longer be evaded, because it is
the object of a direct intuition and the substance of all
knowledge."[11]

What we now seek, then, is what John Calvin called
"the regeneration of the Spirit," and what Jonathan
Edwards called "a new kind of perception or spiritual
sensation," as different from the outer "as the sweet
taste of honey is diverse from the ideas men get of
honey by only looking on and feeling it."[12] In the words
of a more contemporary spokesman, what we are looking for are "the kinds of knowledge by which man loves
and aspires and perseveres and trusts," the kinds that
nourish his wisdom beyond science and his actions
"beyond the diktats of blind nature," the kinds that
leave his mind open to the possibility of "ultimate
mystery."[13] Or in terms of the ethic of care, "we are
ultimately at home not through dominating or explain-
ing or appreciating things, but through caring and
being cared for."[14]

The older ethic of righteousness looks different in the
light of the newer imperative of caring. They have in
common a concern for neighbor that begins within.
Much of the conventional Puritan ethic must now be put
aside: the eliteness of the saints, the too-easy jump from
sainthood to property accumulation, the tendency to
overstructure our response to grace in terms of work,
church order, and superpatriotism. But in our present
yearning for new spiritual and moral roots, we can
surely profit from the older notion that a right will,
touched with the lovingkindness of benevolent deity,

and set within a land of immense possibilities, is a prime basis of community. The test of the right will henceforth must be concern for others, not the accumulation of goods.

The ethic of righteousness also reminds us that a rightly disposed inner sense has to be expressed through outer, public structures.

Such seers of a new age as Theodore Roszak have proposed that "we should undertake to repeal urban-industrialism as the world's dominant style of life."[15] A group of Florida college students tried repealing the modern world. But the experience was disillusioning. They set out to live to themselves for a while, without technology, to do all of the housework, cooking, and washing by hand, and to provide food by foraging and fishing. The women felt at the end of the experiment that they had been treated "subserviently," and the men felt that their masculinity had been overtested in the task. They turned out to be not very good at fishing by primitive methods.[16] However burdensome and overbearing the structures of technology (and the state) might seem today, we cannot do without them and still preserve an ethic of shared living. Here is where some of the alternate approaches to community fail. "Structurelessness" can be a tyranny, too: "The end of consciousness-raising leaves people with no place to go and the lack of structure leaves them with no way of getting there."[17]

No community can survive without "associations" (MacIver) to express its needs and purposes. And that is just the point: from now on, we must make our institutions express the benefits of interdependence—and not let them dominate us. This may well mean "stepping down the technological scale" so that we once again experience each other—and in fact recover the sense of what it is to "experience" someone or something at all.

"One of the most subtle dehumanizing things technology does is to eliminate experience," argues George
Nelson. As a student, Nelson went on a bicycle trip in
the Italian hills. Here was a situation in which the tool
did not overwhelm the man, for he could remember
"that I walked up a lot of hills." There were other things
to remember: how his appetite grew, how sleeping was
no problem, and how it felt "trying to beat a thunder-
storm down a ten-mile hill to Perugia late one afternoon." He adds: "I don't think there would have been
that much to remember with a car."[18]

Technology, along with the state, makes up the outer
membrane of that organic whole that we call society. As
Daniel J. Boorstin aptly puts it, "Edison . . . was not
simply 'inventing' a new incandescent bulb, he was organizing a new electric lighting system for whole
communities."[19] For this very reason, one can argue
that technology, despite the ills it has brought us, can
itself undergo the same change of identity that we have
symbolized as a process of initiation. Kenneth Vaux
urges that religious vision and technological planning
interpenetrate each other, that if we act within a
framework of hope, we may seek to employ technology
to meliorate "alienations of modern man." In the realm
of health, for example, religious hope points to "an all-
out effort to defeat those forces that inflict disease, de-
bilitation and death." To be sure, in developing medical
technology we are bound to err, fall into hubris and
blasphemy. Yet care requires the effort and the risk:
"We cannot rest while one still suffers or dies who would
not suffer or die if we cared."[20]

Technological innovation is relentless. The question
is not whether it will occur, but how it is to be bent and
shaped by human initiative. There can be no turning
back. Opponents of abortion will be dismayed, for example, that successively simpler methods of terminating

pregnancies have been developed over the past few
years, to the extent that one of the latest has become
known as "lunch-hour abortion." But what of the simul-
taneous development, a product of the same relentless
effort, that saw a new, simpler and cheaper kidney
purifying machine put on the market? The new
machine would cost less than $5,000. It could use ordi-
nary tap water and be operated at home. Its developer
predicted that it would greatly benefit children and
older patients with heart or blood vessel disease, and
might even be used by persons living alone.[21]

In the same way, the machinery of the state can be an
expression of community purpose. Big government in
our day has grossly exceeded this assignment and
abused it, to be sure. Still, there are signs of change.
When Denver citizens turned down a chance to have the
Winter Olympics because they feared the effect on their
environment, they were expressing an ethic of interdependence. The legislature of Oregon has had the Wil-
lamette River cleaned up. In more than a dozen states,
new laws forbid stores to discriminate against women in
offering credit. New York's state bank superintendent
called on all state-chartered lending institutions to
abolish sex discrimination in selecting loan applicants.[22]

Where the pressure is off, the commitment to interdependence is even clearer, and may be a sign of what
can be hoped for elsewhere. The nations have agreed to
dedicate the continent of Antarctica to peaceful studies,
for example, and that commitment has been honored.
As a symbol, each year since 1957 a Soviet scientist has
settled in for a stay at one of the American research
bases, and an American scientist has spent time at one of
the Soviet stations. "The result is another important
antarctic achievement—the realization that, in a part of
the globe where all the elements are pitted against them,

men can work together to understand and overcome
their common problems."[23]

Finally, the Puritan heritage prompts us to ask one
more set of questions: What of the religious tradition
itself in this country? How can it help us toward caring
and toward community? What of the churches today?
How can they help?

A friend of mine—we'll call her Norma McCall—not
long ago went through a tough experience. She was
beaten for re-election to the school board. Four years
earlier, the voters had swept a progressive board, including Norma, into office. Now, just as decisively, they
swept them out and put in a more standpat group of
trustees.

Shortly after the election Norma and I had a talk.
Understandably hurt and bewildered, she was nonetheless already bouncing back. She spoke with high interest
about her current work on a grand jury. She had agreed
to go on the boards of several volunteer groups.

Norma, a serious believer (Protestant), exemplifies
something central to my understanding of faith. For
me, her rapid bounce-back summed up one of the great
strengths of the religious heritage I speak of.

The reason I am a Christian, I think, is that the Christian faith teaches me that I have a new chance every day.
Everything comes back offered anew. Reversal, defeat,
sloppiness, selfishness—these cursed parts of living may
have fouled things up right down to the present moment, but there is a new chance here and now to step
out afresh.

Though I am talking about the future—how things
can be new, how hopes can come up again, how the
offer is always open—I am still talking about the past, a
tradition, a heritage. Though I am talking about a new
chance, I am still talking about an old understanding.

Like the perverse Houston voters who voted Norma
out, we human beings can take only so much initiation
at a time. Sometimes we won't budge, and even go
backwards. But there is still this tradition, this faith, that
goes back to others, long before me, who believed, and
acted on it, that all things could, and would, be made
new.

What is always being renewed is the chance to care.
The tradition shows me that it is not an accidental opportunity or a whim of mine. It is part of a covenant.

What about the churches? Are they really carrying
out this tradition? Are they really helping us to hope
and are they really holding out new chances to care?

For the Puritans the church was the indispensable
institution that nurtured the impulse to community.
Given the new spiritual yearnings that we have been
examining, we might suppose that a new day for organized religion might be thinkable. But like the agencies
of the state, the churches in our day have lost much
of the people's confidence. There is unquestionably a
spitirual thirst going begging right now. I honestly cannot blame my students when they turn to yet another
guru or to a new Jesus cell—even though I don't think
they will find what they are looking for there, either.
(It is much as Francine du Plessix Gray put it: "Here
are the Seventies—a procession of revivalist, consciousness-raising, sensitivity session rock extravaganzas in
divine duds. . . . I feel sick."[24])

But there are signs in the churches, there are signs.
Mostly for fun I asked my class at Rice to go into small
groups and come up with a list of a dozen authentic
American heroes. Then I gave the same assignment to a
lay study group at a nearby church.

Though the church people were more or less what
you'd expect—affluent, settled, coats and ties—they
came up, in my judgment, with a better list than my
students did, for it showed new potential for caring.

The church folk put two blacks—Martin Luther King Jr. and Jackie Robinson—on their list. They also listed women—Susan B. Anthony, for example. My students listed not a black, not a woman. They stuck mainly to presidents, frontiersmen, and Jim Thorp.

A better hero-list doesn't say the churches have turned around yet, of course. Their work is cut out for them. I think they know what needs to be done. They have to bite the bullet in the same way, say, that the public library in my city has just done. For years libraries were "seen" as places where books were guarded and secreted. Users of the books were suspect. But our library, in a new burst of consciousness, is working hard to help people find out about things they want to know, actually pressing books on them, putting forward the invitation to use its facilities in an almost insistent way. Here is a new awareness of what is at the heart of being a library, a new sense of direction, a new "intentionality," as the phenomenologists would say. It is no longer a matter of locking up books, it is now a matter of getting people to read and use them.[25]

The ethic of interdependence and care represents a challenge of like sort to the churches: To be henceforth less those centers where people come to show how respectable, reserved, and well off they are. To be a new kind of center where men and women can take off their masks and try out the strange new world of caring.

It is the churches of the land, in spite of all, that have kept the idea of the Gospel alive in its truest, deepest sense. Theirs has been the message of the most profound initiation of all. It is found in both Hebrew Bible and New Testament:

"The Spirit of the Lord is upon me,
because he has anointed me to preach good news to the poor.
He has sent me to proclaim release to the captives
and recovering of sight to the blind,

to set at liberty those who are oppressed,
to proclaim the acceptable year of the Lord."

—Luke 4:18–19 (quoting Isaiah 61:1–2)

The American people have never been more in need
of good news, both about their hearts and about their
country. It is a rare opportunity for the churches.
Courageously seized, it could both renew religion and
help us all toward restored community.

VARIATIONS ON A THEME BY WHITEY

We have now and then considered comic strip characters as types of the American hero. But another way of
seeing them is to take them as counselors or teachers,
pointing the way to a new configuration of community.

Thus in *Doonesbury*, Rufus, a black youth who sometimes prefers to be called "Thor," is the ferryman across
the river of racial diversity for his let's-do-better white
pals. One day Rufus decides to escort a trio of them on a
guided tour of the ghetto.

First off, Rufus and his wards run into some local
street friends of Rufus'. In standard militant style the
friends want to know from him what is with his
group—"what's happening here, man?"

The whites with Rufus cut in and sophomorically try
out their idea of Afro language, just to show they're
with it ethnic-wise. They use expressions like "All
power, fellas," "Check it out," and, of course, the pre-
dictable, "Right on."

The blacks glare. Guide Rufus turns edgy. Then
what? Do knives appear? Not at all. The blacks break up
laughing at Doonesbury and Co.

Another fascinating new face is that of Lt. Flap, a
cool, confident, stylishly Afro'd company grade officer

in *Beetle Bailey*. General Halftrack, who in standard American hero lore should be the authority figure, is instead an ineffectual but good-natured plodder, never quite in the know. The general leads his men on field maneuvers. He decides to telephone his officers in various sectors to see how things are going. He gets to Lt. Flap. How's the situation? asks the general.

"Real cool," replies the unflappable Flap. "We're getting it together." The general turns to an aide and orders him to "Find out what Flap's men are building and take some blankets with you."

Both these examples make the same point. Whitey is in a new situation. He must at least try to understand another world, another vocabulary, and he cannot lightly take it over and make it his own. He must reckon with it for what it is. He must grant the reality of varying forms and notions of what it means to be an American.

Of first importance in the renewed American myth is the ethic of justice, dissent, and reform, the serious decline of which we have already chronicled. Now it is possible to see some of the reasons for the decline, and how out of apparent morbidity may come new life.

The ethic of the "rights of man" was articulated in America by and for people of British stock. For this nascent American ethic to become a saving myth for all of us it had first to be wrenched from the ethnocentricity of its origins. The first solution was to admit to the club anyone willing or able to become an honorary WASP.

Now that solution has been challenged. Protestant thought control and the King James Bible have been removed from classrooms by Supreme Court decisions. Good schools have been opened to all. Catholics, blacks, and women have begun to enter the national imperium on their own terms.

One effect is a more visible "centeredness" in the

spirit of minority groups. In Bernard Malamud's novel, *The Tenants,* Willie Spear, the would-be black novelist, is locked in continual conflict-and-communication with Harry Lesser, a Jewish writer who finds it easier to work on his unfinishable book than to be a human being. Willie sums up his resolve to be himself, over against Lesser, and to be a writer about the black experience: "I believed in my blackness."[26] This return to confidence in one's ethnic origins has spread. Among Hispanic-Americans, for example, it is a question of language and cultural history as well as racial identity.

Though the Anglo-Saxon stock in America is still the largest, it is now the largest *minority.* Commenting on the diversity of Americans that candidates for president must now face, Theodore H. White points out that the original British-Protestant culture did furnish the basic framework of American "values, customs, sports, laws, education." If this older culture continues to be "the matrix into which all other cultures fit," still things have changed, for "this mortar, which cements the other cultures into the political tradition, grows always thinner." The added cultural inputs come to mind: Germans, blacks, Irish, Poles, Russians, Yugoslavs, Czechs, Swedes, Norwegians, Finns, Danes, Italians, French, Belgians, Dutch; people of Hispanic origin; Jews, increasing numbers of Chinese, Japanese, and other orientals.[27]

Thus the American myth of the rights of man, though it may have been born of a local claim about the "rights of Englishmen," is now undergoing the transforming power of the rite of initiation and now underwrites a deeper freedom—the freedom to live out the distinctive texture of one's own share of the heritage, be that texture Afro-American, Franco-Catholic, overall-freak, or Wall Street-gray. And a new meaning is given to the ideal of "equality," which basically comes to us out

of the older justice ethic: in a new America where interdependence is recognized, it allows for living variations
on the theme of what it means to live in dignity as a
human being.

Another emphasis of the older justice ethic, we may
recall, was the push toward reform, and the gospel of
progress. Here, too, the re-emergence of the ideal from
the ashes of dead community occurs, but the result is a
new form.

Part of the decline of community in America is really
the decline of *hopes* for community. After so many years
of progress of all sorts, the institutions of the country
still do not serve the people very well. The cities are in
some ways tougher to live in than ever. Progress came,
but it was uneven, and too often misdirected toward
new highway systems rather than toward new incre-
ments in human dignity.

In a day when care amid interdependence is a higher
heroic virtue than asphalting new acres of former wil-
derness, the notion of progress must be revised. Progress now means tackling present institutions and over-
hauling them. Reform means creating new situations in
which human dignity may be spread around. Technology, preferably of a bit lower wattage henceforth, can
now best be used for humanizing the cities. The motivation and wherewithal for these advances need not
necessarily be sought first at the level of the Federal
government. Nashville has put in an imaginative gar-
bage-burning plant that will furnish energy downtown (thus making a dent in two crises) without any
Federal funds at all. Much of the challenge, and responsibility, may fairly be said now to lie with lesser loci
of moving and shaking—with localities, churches, and
individuals.

The disillusionment with governmental action and
with many of our institutions that has grown in recent

years is not all bad. With decline of confidence in institutions has come, fortunately, a heightening of the spirit of personal responsibility. "Respect for the rights of others has never been higher than today," was the comment of Lou Harris, the authority on public opinion, in an otherwise somber interview by A.B.C. newsman Howard K. Smith.[28] From the perspective of an ethic of interdependence and care, this gives a new impetus to the idea of "progress."

Where the two values of dignity and progress threaten to conflict, perhaps dignity henceforth should get more of the benefit of the doubt. Such conflicts arise constantly nowadays in, say, medical ethics. Should an aged, terminally ill person be permitted to die as a man or woman of sense and initiative, or should his life be technically prolonged, even though the tubes and valves hooked to his body rob him of these attributes?

In Houston, during the heyday of the heart-transplant era, a famed four-way transplant took place at one large hospital. From the same donor came the heart, a lung, and both kidneys.

The process of getting the donor organs undoubtedly raised the most delicate questions of human dignity, not for the fatally injured Mexican-American woman who became the donor, but for her family. The woman was already "neurologicially dead," though her body could artifically be kept respiring. The husband and other close relatives, understandably taking a natural, layman's attitude, interpreted the respiration as a sign of life.

For more than an hour the doctor talked with the husband, attempting to explain what "neurologically dead" meant, while the family, as Thomas Thompson recounts it, "flocked about answering in Spanish and English." The husband was finally persuaded to have his wife transferred to the big hospital in the medical center where the transplant team waited. The doctor promised to have another EEG done there. "Gonzalez nodded; in one hour he had learned what brain waves are and how they govern the destiny of the earthly soul."[29]

What if Gonzalez had refused? Should he and his family then have been criticized? Not for standing in the way of medical "progress," I should say. If at all, for an entirely different reason, for failing to sense their interdependence with the four other human beings waiting for transplants.

How will men face the future, when they are guided by a genuine sense of interdependence? Surely they can build on the example set by the justice-seekers up to now. The view of justice that has prevailed in this country has furnished the insight that present community is always inadequate; that past models and present understandings may have to be replaced to give further room for the human prospect in the future. "No society can make a perpetual constitution, or even a perpetual law," argued Thomas Jefferson. "The earth belongs always to the living generation."[30] He thought leeway must be left for future generations to dispose of the benefits of earth as they see fit.

But this forward-running spirit of American life, as we have already seen, tends to devolve into something more like feathering one's own nest for coming times, rather than "freeing up" community for its future members. Now the time has come to move to—or return to—a more radical sense of the future—a future in which we imagine ourselves as obligated to care for those who have not yet been born.

That spirit is already implied in Jefferson's belief that "the earth belongs in usufruct to the living." The idea is not that we are therefore free to do anything we want with the earth, but precisely the opposite, that we are obligated to pass it all along unhampered, unencumbered, and if possible, enhanced, to posterity.

Even our best intentions toward the future have not ordinarily, encompassed this more radical idea. Our received notion of equality, for example, has been mainly concentrated upon taking in those who are with us today. But Jørgen Randers calls for the idea to be expanded, by a leap of the moral consciousness, to include those, say, "who are going to live on our planet over the next 200 years." We still find this hard to imagine because our tendency is to "essentially assign zero value to anything happening more than twenty years from now."

Christianity made a great leap forward, says Randers: it raised a new ideal, condemning selfish gratification, and calling for "consideration for the welfare of all people living at the same point in time." But now this ideal has to be expanded:

Basically we are facing only one ethical question in the pending global crisis. This is to decide on whether we want to continue to let our actions be guided by the short-term . . . , or whether we should adopt a longer-term perspective.[31]

The "we-relation" that is the building block of community now has to be thought to include future partners, not just present ones. The notion of care must be understood as really directed at *all* the others—that is, including those who will live beyond the limits of one's own generation. That is really what Thomas Jefferson was getting at when he proposed that laws expire after thirty-four years—the length of time of one generation. In the new era, then, the challenge of interdependence and the imperative of care point us toward a far more radical idea of the future than we are used to—but it is an idea that was implicitly present in our heritage from the start.

With these changes, the spirit of the older justice ethic is both restored and reshaped—in a new sense of equality, a more care-oriented version of progress, and a more radical sense of our covenant with future men and women. It is also obvious that the spirit of "feisty dissent" that we have talked about as characterizing the older justice ethic will still be appropriate in a new ethic of care. The old cause of human dignity and human rights is still there, even if emerging in new forms. There will always be a place for the old American sense of outrage at injustice and of impassioned action for a just community.

What am I asking you to do, as a reader of this book, and as a fellow advocate of the dignity of man? The first call upon all of us is to *accept* something, rather than to *do* anything. What we are called on to *do* is to *accept* our new identity as Americans.

Things are different. Maybe we need a new name of some kind to point it up. The biblical Abram, father of Israel, after covenanting anew with God, is so changed that he now is called something else: "No longer shall your name be Abram, but your name shall be Abraham" (Genesis 17:5). Red Little, undergoing a momentous change of identity, remains true to his people, but he becomes Malcolm X. His people, within a decade, cast off older names because of their strides forward and take on a new one: from Negroes and colored, to blacks.

Whatever our new identity may look like in detail, it will have a central feature. It will mark us as men and women who, acknowledging our heritage, now count caring for others as the highest test of that heritage.

I have talked much about mythology, rites of passage, and initiation. The point was not to promote the scientific study of mythology. It was instead to search for a way to convey my belief that death throes may be the forerunner of new life, that bad times in America may yield to better days. What do I ask of you? Don't cut and run. Instead, bet on the republic. We don't have to excuse injustice and misgovernment to do that. Cover your bet by doing something for justice, for widening the scope. Put those who would lead to the tests of initiation. In this country, the franchise says that we are our own medicine men, it is we who "separate the men from the boys." We are past the tribal ritual of knocking out the candidate's tooth, as with the Australian aborigines, but we can and should be tough-minded when it comes to selecting those who are to run the country.

Above all we should remember that state and country exist to serve community, and not the other way around.

NEW CUP, NEW CAUSE

Houston's Montrose area was once a fashionable residential section, with block after block of elegant town houses. But the "better" suburbs followed a rapid line of march to the westward, and Montrose became a transitional neighborhood. In the last few years it has taken on a new identity: the old homes have been turned into restaurants (some fashionable, some of more populist character), craft shops, book stores, and sidewalk cafes. Montrose is a center for the young and free, for pot smokers, for the tank-top subculture, for gourmets, for middle-aged, part-time hippies, for devotees of the astrological and of the occult.

And it is also the home of a new commune—a term not embraced by its leaders. It is a commune with a difference.

Like the classical communes we discussed in earlier chapters, this one is based on voluntary, intensive mutual existence. But every member of it has at least one major tie to the outside world: to be in the group, each person must be a medical or paramedical worker of some kind, or be a relative of a member who is.

They call themselves a "medical community," and also "a local body of Christ"—though they do not think of themselves as a church. Indeed, they belong to a variety of churches. One of the members is a Catholic priest (who is required by his bishop, however, to sleep elsewhere, in a Catholic diocese-owned house).

One of the leaders, a Houston physician known as "Dr. Bob," explained the group's reason for being: "Our calling is to be medical people and return the life that God gives us not only to our patients but to our profession." Thus, alongside the classical trait, for communes, of a close-knit voluntary basis, this group displays a variant trait: it is not a "do your own thing" group; it has not turned its back on an evil world; it is not retreating from society, disillusioned, to the isolation of the fringes.

Another variation from the traditional image of a commune is the life-style of the members. There is no official list of moral rules, but emphasis instead upon what the individuals in the group believe the Bible leads them to do. They have some people who smoke. Some, if not most, have been known to take a glass of wine, a beer, or a mixed drink.

There are binding features in good communal style, however. The members live together, of course—in houses furnished them by a private foundation whose interest, it seems, was in preserving the old homes of the Montrose area. All members work, or are related to members who work, at an inner-city clinic that has become a ministry to poverty-stricken people. Members share cars, money, even personal items like toothpaste. They have common worship. Their motivation is based on the idea that Christians share lives and possessions fully.

And they are bound together by an outward-looking purpose. "The community is a launching pad for a more powerful ministry in the field of medicine," says Dr. Bob.[32]

Here we can see a key shift in communal living patterns illustrative of an ethic of interdependence. The voluntary gathering that constitutes the community does not hermetically seal it off from the world and from service. The "common cup" is a rally point for serving rather than for withdrawal.

Jay and Heather Ogilvy, in a report on their own experience of communal living in New Haven, endorse a similar idea, the "pluralistic commune." Like others seeking the reality of encounter in voluntary groups, they had to face the question: "What about outside connections? Is the expectation that the commune should monopolize our social life?" Their prospective group, while "seeking a network of relationships" among like-minded people, nonetheless was "not planning the rural agrarian trip," and included among its members several graduate students and professionals. The answer came: "We unanimously willed to maintain all of our outside contacts and share them with others in the commune."

Naturally, there were problems to be faced. Those other contacts inevitably represented a threat from, as well as an opening to, the rest of the world. But the Ogilvys have no hesitation in speaking out for the pluralistic commune in preference to the suffocating concept of "we precious few." The pluralistic commune "is a living lesson in tolerance for its members, both with respect to one another and with respect to the 'outside world.'" It is not easy to carry on such a community, with its tensions between inward loyalties and outward openness. "The model is complex, but so is life . . . . we know the pluralistic commune as an intensely living experience."[33]

The important thing is that the members find a "common cause"—a second crucial attribute for communities expressive of the ethic of encounter. To strengthen the commonalty of voluntary association, the group gives itself over to work and to a vision. Here, too, we will find that the recognition of interdependence will open new possibilities to the encounter-minded. Indeed, the new understanding of the "common cup" that we have just explored—a community that, however tightly united internally, is open to outside service—already points the way toward new possibilities for the "common cause."

What is the plausible new cause in an era of interdependence? It is to point to the "Good News" that we have been talking about—the best bet for community in this day of confusion, when old and new heroes, old and new conceptions of American life, old and new versions of community are vying with each other. If the new ethic of care is still only a David facing a Goliath, nevertheless its adherents know it bears the burden of the future. What is needed are seed communities, or to use an image from the American revolution, "committees of correspondence," to witness to the new idea, to look to "the creation of flesh-and-blood alternatives to the mainstream pattern of life."[34]

Here lies work and vision aplenty for new communities based on the reality of encounter. I can see three aspects of this new service:

First, groups are needed as models to show what personal encounter might look like in a day of interdependence.

The newspapers are full nowadays of accounts of "breakaway" persons, school boards, congregations, and even cities, and the withdrawals often look more like retreats from the human network than like new ways of serving it. Here is a town of 650 in South Dakota, in which the school board orders a novel burned. Naturrally, that decision gets nationwide publicity. The townspeople react angrily. Said one woman: "This was not meant to be nationwide. It was for our little town. We have our standards and we will stick to them. The others can do what they want."[35] This kind of turning aside is no longer saving to the human prospect, if it ever was. Can the new encounter ethic give rise to counter-communities—these, too, with "standards" that they will stick to—showing a better sense of care?

Second, intensive groups are still needed to stand, like the early Christians, over against "Caesar"—meaning now not only heavy-handed governance but also overbearing commercial hegemony. In the past, the members of such groups could draw their strength from each other, and conserve that strength by sealing themselves off from society. The Mennonites and Amish of former days, and many of their contemporary successsors, are examples. But in a day of interdependence, the witness against Caesar must be more complex. Perhaps a better model for us is the figure of the exiled Russian novelist, Aleksandr Solzhenitsyn, who risked liberty and life to communicate through his writings, and whose message included the drawing of a distinction between his country and the state—a point that has eluded a good many Americans on both right and left. Solzhenitsyn's recent *Gulag Archipelago* tells of the mistreatment of citizens, the dehumanizing of the Russian people (or attempts at it) under the Soviet state. To be published it had to be smuggled out to the West. This was done by "a network of people who know each other, travel, meet, and have in common the love of Russia." Eventually what the book says will become known to the Russian people.[36]

Third, some groups bonded together through encounter can find "common cause" in affirming the new American identity that is emerging. For a long time now, the point had to be made negatively: that community has been lost, that America has lost sight of its goals, and so forth. I have collected numerous examples of this negative witness in earlier parts of this book.

Now the new identity is emerging and can be pointed to. What is needed are committed voluntary groups to embrace and tell the message: America, thank heaven, is at last going interdependent. In the last decade there were communes whose members shut themselves off in protest against an obnoxious distortion of the American dream. Now there is another kind of call—for groups to explore and proclaim the new possibilities in America.

So far we have been examining the possible outlines of a new voluntary group idea in a day of emergent interdependence. But let us also recall that the spirit of the older encounter ethic could exist in society at large, among individuals, as well as in gathered cells. So can it be for the new American idea: its meaning, too, can be explored and carried out in diverse personal relationships today.

A few weeks ago, I ran into a young couple in the laundry room. They had just moved into the Bellefontaine. From the way they were dressed, I had imagined what they were like. "America-haters, I daresay," said I to myself. One can fill in the details as to wardrobe: wire glasses, long dress, no shoes—the girl. Sleeveless net top, grubby jeans, sandals—the boy. We exchanged pleasantries, and the girl asked me for the time.

"Can I ask you for just one more thing?" she said as I was going out the door with my washed and dried laundry.

"Yeh, sure," said I. (Here's the seasoned teacher who's heard it all from negative kids.)

"Will you pray for America?" From the way she said

it, I knew that she was around the corner. It was no longer *Amerika* that she was talking about.

In Connecticut a science teacher found that his eighth-graders—children of their times, legatees of Vietnam—refused to salute the flag or recite the pledge of allegiance. The teacher stood alone and did so. One day, finally, one boy joined in.

The teacher began to read to his students, things like the writings of Thomas Wolfe and some of the things John F. Kennedy had said. He came to an excerpt from Wolfe's "The Promise of America"—a part about every man with his chance, "his shining, golden opportunity." It spoke of a person's right to be himself, to become whatever "his vision" could make him. That day, all but one of the students stood up to recite the pledge with him.[37] Perhaps it was a good thing that there was still one hold-out. That shows nobody *has* to do it.

The older encounter ethic offered us the vision that *living, present* personal relationships are the essence of community. However important the past—our roots and our heritage; however important the future—our hopes and our destiny; the center of meaning is *now,* in our mutual presence to one another. An ethic of care elaborates that very theme:

> In the broad sense, "being with" characterizes the process of caring itself: in caring for another person we can be said to be basically with him in his world, in contrast to simply knowing about him from outside.[38]

The scope of an ethic of caring reaches out beyond mere face-to-face sharing to being with others in broader configurations and interactions. Voluntary groups and intense, saving personal relationships, yes. But also voluntary groups that are permeable to the network of others beyond; they need us, and we need them. Encounter in private modes, yes—everyone needs that sometime. But let us also have encounter as care for others beyond the pale of our private lives, encounter with others regardless of nationality, encounter of men with their country and its meaning, and of their country with other countries. These are the initiatives called for now.

THE NEW AMERICAN COMMUNITY

The *Christian Century* asked assorted American leaders to suggest ways of celebrating our national bicentennial. Theologian Harvey Cox wrote in to say he thought we should "spend the next 100 years celebrating the world and the neighborhood." But not the nation itself—which in the form of the state represents "a misleading level of belonging." He proposed "individual street fairs and neighborhood world fairs," and that we begin "putting political *power* at those levels also."[39]

Until we all go on Greenwich Mean Time, however, we cannot refuse responsibility to the national level. True, the problems and hopes are universal: food, fuel, fighting, justice, dignity, peace. We will have to have world approaches if we are to have local solutions. But the very talk we bring to the problems, the very moral patterns we act out of, the very traditions that shape our thoughts, even the hopes we move ahead with, are intensively shaped by our homelands.

To follow Cox' suggestion would be to surrender the country to those grim souls with the LOVE IT OR LEAVE IT bumper stickers. It would be to leave it. It would be to yield unchecked, uncontested power to the state: the opposite of his wish.

We do not "belong" to the state. It "belongs" to us. Too many theologians, rightly appalled by recent abuse of power in the White House, forget there is a distinction between one's government and his country, between the state and one's community.

But I can understand why Cox feels the way he does.

The loss of a sense of community in America is real, as we have seen. It is painful, and it leaves us poorer. But it is not the end of the world. In primitive life, loyalty to the tribe was strong and uninterrupted because there were no options, there was nowhere else to go. Myths that led to confidence in the tribe's gods and its destiny drew allegiance not as the best choices, but as the fundamental structure of reality, and an alternate life style was unthinkable. The twentieth century could go back to that kind of nation and community only in such aberrations as Nazism. To the extent that patriotism in America has now and again echoed this tribal level, we can be glad we are past it and into an era of more critical allegiance.

No face-to-face or local community can be healthy, however, if it feels no pull from a wider context. For their own good, Americans must risk again the leap of commitment outward, from their private loyalties back to the national community, and beyond that, to a renewed moral investment, however risky, in the community of nations.

Of the first importance in this outward movement are two challenges, both of which have emerged in the course of our study:

First, let us accept the new identity that is offered us. Interdependence and care are the clues to it.

Second, let us rescue the older myths upon which community was built, reinterpreting them for our crisis and for our new identity, retelling them with help from those who have seen beyond the death throes.

The Declaration of Independence, for example, needs to be reworked by a new generation of artists and story-tellers, as drastically overhauled, say, as the Gospels were in *Jesus Christ Superstar*. Similarly, a new translation must be found for the original Puritan trust in divine initiative, and in the promise of a right will to order a good community. And new ways must be sought of combining the excitement of personal encounter with a vision that includes us all.

The first idea of community in America had to be built up, haltingly, out of promise and crisis—by the colonists, our forebears. There were "periods of decline interspersed with periods of incline and rapid breakthrough." The colonists had to "learn" to call their homeland "America," as they replaced one set of symbolic meanings with another.[40] Now we face the same process of learning, or relearning, to call ourselves a community. Half of alienation is believing that nothing can be done. Half of restoration is taking up the symbols—new and old—that will let us believe better of ourselves.

It is not an easy thing to live out a new identity in an age when community at every level, from local to national, has seemed dead or dying. But we can begin with Thomas Jefferson, who wrote this from France to his daughter, Martha: "It is part of the American character to consider nothing as desperate; . . . we are obliged to invent and execute; to find means within ourselves."[41] The new American myth tells us once again that we are better off when "we mutually pledge to each other our lives, our fortunes, and our sacred honor." It points to a reborn, if more modest, love of country, and to a restored, if different, sense of community; to new "warming fires."

Notes

CHAPTER I

1. *Time*, September 25, 1972, p. 5.
2. *Saturday Review: The Society*, April 21, 1973, pp. 61–66.
3. *Nashville Tennessean*, March 5, 1972.
4. *Houston Chronicle*, February 6, 1972.
5. *Houston Chronicle*, July 1, 1973.
6. *Newsweek*, July 16, 1973, p. 52.
7. *Newsweek*, July 16, 1973, pp. 53, 57.
8. *Newsweek*, April 24, 1972, p. 65.
9. New York: World Publishing Co., 1971; *Houston Chronicle*, March 26, 1972.
10. *Houston Chronicle*, July 1, 1973.
11. *Christian Science Monitor*, April 21, 1973.
12. *New York Times*, April 16, 1973, pp. 1, 46. In Los Angeles County, the youth suicide rate doubled in a decade. For Los Angeles, the rate for males ten to nineteen years of age grew from 3.3 per hundred thousand to 10. Among those 20 to 29 the rate went from 18.9 to 41.3. Among females the corresponding figures were an increase from .04 to 8 for those

10–19 years of age, and from 6.3 to 26.2 for those 20–29 years of age.

13. *Houston Post,* June 21, 1973. For many more illustrations of the decline of community in America, see Ralph Keyes, *We, the Lonely People: Searching For Community* (New York: Harper & Row, 1973).

CHAPTER II

1. *Houston Chronicle,* July 15, 1972.
2. Bernard Malamud, *The Tenants* (New York: Pocket Books, 1972), p. 208; Gabriel Marcel, *Being and Having,* tr. Katherine Farrer (Westminster, England: Dacre, 1949).
3. Alfred Schutz, *Collected Papers,* II, ed. Arvid Brodersen (The Hague: Martinus Nijhoff, 1964), pp. 24–25.
4. Ibid., p. 29.
5. Ibid., p. 31.
6. Ibid., p. 38.
7. Robert M. MacIver, *On Community, Society and Power,* ed. Leon Bramson (Chicago: University of Chicago Press, 1970), pp. 29–31; my italics.
8. Ibid., p. 40.
9. The term *ethic* must be distinguished from *ethics* (with an "s"). The latter term refers to the *process* of thinking about and appraising the cluster of values and moral patterns that constitutes an ethic. An ethic is related to ethics in the same way that a myth is related to mythology. For further discussion of American myths, see the following chapter. For further discussion of American ethics, i.e., the process, see Chapter V.
10. Bernard Malamud, *A New Life* (New York: Dell, 1963).
11. Jonathan Edwards, *Treatise Concerning the Religious Affections* (London: Banner of Truth Trust, 1961), *Select Works,* III, p. 169.
12. Edwards, *Religious Affections,* p. 320.
13. Edwards, *The Nature of True Virtue* (Ann Arbor: University of Michigan Press, 1960), p. 86.
14. "The interest of righteousness in the commonwealth and

holiness in the Churches are inseparable . . . Christ reigns among us in the commonwealth as well as in the Church and hath his glorious interest involved and wrapt up in the good of both societies respectively."—Uriah Oakes, Cambridge clergyman and sometime president of Harvard in *New England Pleaded With* (1673), cited in Sydney E. Ahlstrom, *A Religious History of the American People* (New Haven: Yale University Press, 1972), p. 149.

15. Kant's philosophy sounds many of these themes in a non-theistic fashion: "Nothing in the world—indeed nothing even beyond the world—can possibly be conceived which could be called good without qualification except a *good will*. . . . The good will is not good because of what it effects or accomplishes or because of its adequacy to achieve some proposed end; it is good only because of its willing, i.e., it is good of itself. . . . Usefulness or fruitlessness can neither diminish nor augment this worth. . . . Fidelity in promises and benevolence on principle . . . have intrinsic worth. . . . their worth consists not in effects. . . . nor in advantage and utility. . . ; it consists only in intentions, i.e., maxims of the will which are ready to reveal themselves in this manner through actions even though success does not favor them. . . . I should never act in such a way that I could not also will that my maxim should be a universal law." Immanuel Kant, *Foundations of the Metaphysics of Morals*, tr. Lewis White Beck (Indianapolis: Bobbs-Merrill, Library of Liberal Arts, 1959), pp. 9, 10, 18, 53.

16. Edwards, *Religious Affections*, pp. 178, 340.

17. Samuel Eliot Morison, *The Oxford History of the American People* (New York: Oxford University Press, 1965), pp. 212–213.

18. Thomas Jefferson, *Life and Selected Writings*, ed. Adrienne Koch and William Peden (New York: Modern Library, 1944), p. 324.

19. Ibid., p. 267.

20. Thomas Paine, *The Age of Reason*, ed. Philip S. Foner (New York: Citadel, 1945), Part I, p. 464.

21. Jefferson, *Life and Selected Writings*, pp. 388–390.

22. Ibid., p. 436.

23. Ibid., p. 324.
24. Ibid., p. 595.
25. Ibid., p. 238.
26. Ibid., pp. 606–607.
27. Abraham Lincoln, *Selected Speeches, Messages, and Letters,* ed. T. Harry Williams (New York: Holt, Rinehart and Winston, 1957), pp. 113, 137.
28. Ibid., p. 72.
29. Jefferson, *Life and Selected Writings,* p. 640.
30. Lincoln, *Selected Speeches, Messages, and Letters,* p. 80.
31. Ibid., p. 50.
32. *The Autobiography of Malcolm X* (New York: Grove, 1966), pp. 366–367.
33. Cf. Stephan Silha in *Christian Science Monitor,* July 16, 1973.
34. Ulrich Stadler, "Cherished Instructions on Sin, Excommunication, and the Community of Goods," in *Spiritual and Anabaptist Writers,* ed. George H. Williams and Angel M. Mergal (Philadelphia: Westminster Press, 1957), pp. 277–284.
35. Ahlstrom, *A Religious History of the American People,* p. 236.
36. Mark Holloway, Introduction to John Humphrey Noyes, *History of American Socialisms* (New York: Dover Publications, 1966), vii.
37. Noyes, *History of American Socialisms,* pp. 623, 625, 634.
38. Ibid., pp. 626, 641–642.
39. Ahlstrom, *A Religious History of the American People,* p. 499.
40. Franklin H. Littell, in Prefatory Essay to Charles Nordhoff, *The Communistic Societies of the United States* (New York: Schocken Books, 1965), xiv. Perhaps we should keep in mind that Nordhoff, who wrote in 1875, as well as Noyes, used the terms "Communism" and "Communistic" in a pre-Marxist sense to mean, roughly, "commune-ism" and "commune-istic."
41. Theodore Roszak, *Where the Wasteland Ends* (New York: Doubleday Anchor Books, 1973), pp. 390–391.
42. Littell, Prefatory Essay, xv.
43. Douglas Sturm, "The Kibbutzim and the Spirit of Israel: An Interpretative Essay," in *The Family, Communes, and Uto-*

pian Societies, ed. Sallie Te Selle (New York: Harper & Row Torchbooks, 1972), pp. 115–116.
44. *Christian Science Monitor,* July 28, 1973.

CHAPTER III

1. Frantz Fanon, *The Wretched of the Earth,* tr. Constance Farrington (New York: Grove Press, 1968), p. 216.
2. *Newsweek,* July 9, 1973, pp. 50, 56; *Houston Post,* January 11, 1974.
3. Jean Anouilh, *Le Voyageur sans Bagages* (n.p.: La Table Ronde, 1958), p. 109 (my translation).
4. Robert T. Francoeur, "Technology and the Future of Human Sexuality," in *To Create a Different Future,* ed. Kenneth Vaux (New York: Friendship Press, 1972), pp. 106, 86, 91.
5. Paul Tillich, *Dynamics of Faith* (New York: Harper & Row Torchbooks, 1957), pp. 42–43.
6. As we shall see in the next chapter, a pathological version of this approach appeared on our national television screens, during the Senate investigation of the Watergate scandals, in the testimony of numerous executives of the White House and of the "Committee to Re-elect the President."
7. I have adapted this story from several versions of the myth that appear in Claude Lévi-Strauss, *The Raw and the Cooked,* tr. John and Doreen Weightman (New York: Harper & Row Torchbooks, 1969), pp. 155–158.
8. Claude Lévi-Strauss, *The Raw and the Cooked,* p. 12.
9. Account based on A. W. Howitt, *The Native Tribes of South-East Australia* (London: Macmillan, 1904), Ch. IX, and on Mircea Eliade, *Rites and Symbols of Initiation,* tr. Willard R. Trask (New York: Harper & Row Torchbooks, 1965), Ch. I. The quoted excerpt is from Howitt, p. 532.
10. Mircea Eliade, *Rites and Symbols of Initiation,* pp. 2, 3. A convincing argument against use of the term "puberty rites" is made by Arnold van Gennep, *The Rites of Passage,* tr. Monika B. Vizedom and Gabrielle L. Caffee (Chicago: University of Chicago Press, 1960), pp. 65–75. From this point on

I shall use the term initiation to mean what Eliade calls puberty rites here.

11. Ibid., p. 3.

12. Joseph L. Henderson and Maud Oakes, *The Wisdom of the Serpent* (New York: Collier Books, 1963), p. 56.

13. Eliade, *Rites and Symbols of Initiation*, p. 135.

14. Jonathan Edwards, *Select Works*, II (n.p.: Banner of Truth Trust, 1959), p. 71.

CHAPTER IV

1. Morris Jastrow and Albert T. Clay, *An Old Babylonian Version of the Gilgamesh Epic* (New Haven: Yale University Press, 1920), pp. 34–38; William Ellery Leonard, *Gilgamesh* (New York: Viking Press, 1934), p. 18. I have treated the epic selectively. Readers with more than a passing interest should consult these sources and also the source given in note 3 below.

2. Leonard, *Gilgamesh,* p. 40.

3. Joseph L. Henderson and Maud Oakes, *The Wisdom of the Serpent* (New York: Collier Books, 1963), p. 168.

4. Henderson-Oakes, *The Wisdom of the Serpent,* p. 57.

5. Charles C. Brewster, quoted in Edward McIrvine *et al., Dialogue on Technology* (Indianapolis: Bobbs-Merrill, 1967), p. 26.

6. Andrew Carnegie, "Wealth," reprinted in *Democracy and the Gospel of Wealth,* ed. Gail Kennedy (Lexington, Mass.: D. C. Heath, 1949, pp. 1–8.

7. Based on feature story by Martha Liebrum, *Houston Post,* February 1, 1973.

8. *New York Times,* December 16, 1972, p. 27; *Newsweek,* March 5, 1973, p. 46.

9. *Time,* June 25, 1973, p. 12; *Christian Science Monitor,* June 21, 1973.

10. *Christian Science Monitor,* June 23, 1973, *Wall Street Journal,* July 9, 1973.

11. James F. Childress, *Civil Disobedience and Political Obligation: A Study in Christian Social Ethics* (New Haven: Yale University Press, 1971), pp. 4, 10, 11.

12. Chapter II, pp. 48–53.

13. *Christian Science Monitor,* July 12, 1973.

14. Walter Rauschenbusch, *Christianity and the Social Crisis,* ed. Robert D. Cross (New York: Harper & Row Torchbooks, 1964), pp. 139, 325.

15. John Dewey, *Reconstruction in Philosophy* (New York: New American Library Mentor Books, 1950), pp. 147, 136.

16. Ibid., p. 137.

17. Ibid., p, 102.

18. *Newsweek,* July 9, 1973, p. 7.

19. Cf. *Newsweek,* August 6, 1973, p. 5.

20. *Christian Science Monitor,* August 2, 1973. In 1972 the president of the Teamsters' Union drew a salary of $125,000, the president of the Operating Engineers salary and allowances of $103,000, the president of the National Maritime Union salary and allowances of $85,000. The president of the United Auto Workers was less handsomely rewarded, having been paid only $38,000, plus expenses of $9,000. *Houston Chronicle,* July 26, 1973.

21. *Houston Chronicle,* July 26, 1973.

22. *Houston Chronicle,* August 6, 1973.

23. *New York Times,* August 5, 1973, p. 1.

24. Interview with Jeannine Swift on KVRL July 29, 1973.

25. *Christian Science Monitor,* June 18, 1973.

26. Joseph Fletcher, *Situation Ethics: The New Morality* (Philadelphia: Westminster, 1966), pp. 77–78, 85.

27. Fletcher, *Situation Ethics,* p. 139.

28. Hannah Arendt, *On Revolution* (New York: Viking, 1965), p. 93.

29. Richard Todd, "Turned-on and Super-Sincere in California," *Harper's,* January, 1967, p. 46.

30. Fred Hechinger, "Sifting Revolution's Ashes for Salvage," *National Observer,* July 14, 1973, p. 24. The "unwarranted retreat" into conservatism has produced a new series of communes based on strict morality and religious affirmations—the so-called "Jesus people," and such groups as the "Children of God."

31. Theodore Roszak, *Where the Wasteland Ends* (New York: Doubleday Anchor Books, 1973), pp. 174–175.

CHAPTER V

1. Ch. Perrault, *Contes* (Paris: Hazan, 1928), *Le Petit Poucet*, pp. 213–233; P. Saintyves, *Les Contes de Perrault et les Récits Parallèles* (Paris: Libraire Critique, 1923), p. 313.
2. Ibid., p. 314.
3. Ibid., p. 317.
4. Kenneth Vaux, "Religious Hope and Technological Planning," in *To Create a Different Future*, ed. Kenneth Vaux (New York: Friendship Press, 1972), p. 120.
5. Abraham Lincoln, *Selected Speeches, Messages, and Letters*, ed. T. Harry Williams (New York: Holt, Rinehart and Winston, 1957), pp. 246–247.
6. Theodore Roszak, *Where the Wasteland Ends* (New York: Doubleday Anchor Books, 1973), pp. 420–421.
7. This account and some later allusions in this chapter are adapted from my editorials in the *Christian Century*, February 21, 1973, p. 232, and June 28, 1972, pp. 703–704.
8. Erik Erickson, *Identity: Youth and Crisis* (New York: W. W. Norton & Co., 1968), pp. 130–131.
9. Ibid., pp. 235, 236, 242.
10. Joseph L. Henderson and Maud Oakes, *The Wisdom of the Serpent* (New York: Collier Books, 1963), pp. 55–56.
11. John Pfeiffer, *The Emergence of Man* (New York: Harper & Row, 1969), p. 420.

CHAPTER VI

1. Norman Mailer, *Of A Fire on the Moon* (New York: New American Library Signet Books, 1971), pp. 372, 279, 280, 287.
2. Lewis Lapham, "What Movies Try to Sell Us," *Harper's*, November, 1971, p. 106.
3. David Denby, "Men Without Women, Women Without Men," *Harper's*, September, 1973, pp. 51–52.
4. *Houston Chronicle*, December 19, 1973.
5. *Parade*, December 17, 1972, p. 5.
6. *Time*, December 17, 1973, p. 4.
7. *Houston Chronicle*, September 19, 1972.

8. *New Orleans States-Item,* August 18, 1973.

9. *Houston Chronicle,* December 2, 1973. Shortly after publication of the recruitment message, Perot's investment firm failed.

10. *Family Circle,* January, 1974, p. 30; the book is *Rosey Grier's Needlepoint for Men* (New York: Walker & Co., 1973).

11. Joseph L. Henderson and Maud Oakes, *The Wisdom of the Serpent* (New York: Collier Books, 1963), p. 60.

12. Ibid., pp. 165–166.

13. Interview with Constance S. Sammis, *Christian Science Monitor,* August 17, 1973.

14. Reinhold Niebuhr, *Moral Man and Immoral Society* (New York: Charles Scribner's Sons, Scribner Library, 1960), xi. The book was first published in 1932.

15. Ivan Illich, "Technology and Conviviality," in *To Create A Different Future,* ed. Kenneth Vaux (New York: Friendship Press, 1972), p. 41.

16. David Holstrom in *Christian Science Monitor,* July 5, 1973.

17. *Houston Post,* June 21, 1973.

18. Ed Townsend in *Christian Science Monitor,* June 23, 1973.

19. *Christian Science Monitor,* August 16, 1973.

20. Alden Whitman in *New York Times,* December 15, 1973, p. 33.

21. Walter Rauschenbusch, *Christianity and the Social Crisis,* ed. Robert D. Cross (New York: Harper & Row Torchbooks, 1964), pp. 265, 268.

22. Martin Buber, *Between Man and Man,* tr. Ronald Gregor Smith (London: Collins Fontana Library, 1963), p. 23.

23. Milton Mayeroff, *On Caring* (New York: Harper & Row Perennial Library, 1971), p. 21 (my emphasis).

CHAPTER VII

1. Anders Nygren, *The Gospel of God,* tr. L. J. Trinterud (Philadelphia: Westminster Press, 1951), pp. 30–31.

2. Howard T. Odum, *Environment, Power and Society* (New York: Wiley-Interscience, 1971), pp. 236, 244, 247.

3. Ted Morgan in *New York Times Magazine,* December 9, 1973, pp. 90–92.

4. Francine du Plessix Gray in *New York Review,* December 13, 1973, p. 36.

5. *Houston Post,* April 12, 1973.

6. Frederick Sontag and John K. Roth, *The American Religious Experience* (New York: Harper & Row, 1972), p. 297.

7. Jacqueline Teare in *Christian Science Monitor,* June 23, 1973.

8. Cited in John Lear, "Where is Society Going? The Search for Landmarks," *Saturday Review,* April 16, 1972, p. 34.

9. Raymond Aron, *Main Currents in Sociological Thought* (London: Weidenfeld and Nicolson, 1965), I, pp. 1–9.

10. Alden Whitman in *New York Times,* December 15, 1973, p. 33.

11. Pierre Teilhard de Chardin, *The Phenomenon of Man* (New York: Harper & Row Torchbooks, 1961), pp. 175, 164, 55.

12. John Calvin, *Institutes of the Christian Religion,* II. VII. 2; Jonathan Edwards, *Treatise Concerning the Religious Affections* (n.p.: Banner of Truth Trust, 1961), *Select Works,* III, 133.

13. Malachi Martin, "The Scientist as Shaman," *Harper's,* March, 1972, p. 61.

14. Milton Mayeroff, *On Caring* (New York: Harper & Row Perennial Library, 1971), p. 76.

15. Theodore Roszak, *Where the Wasteland Ends* (New York: Doubleday Anchor Books, 1973), p. 380.

16. Interview, *Today,* N.B.C., December 27, 1973.

17. Jo Freeman, "The Tyranny of Structurelessness," *MS,* July, 1973, pp. 87–88.

18. George Nelson, "Design: Great Writers," *Harper's,* April, 1973, p. 48.

19. Daniel J. Boorstin, *The Americans: The Democratic Experience* (New York: Random House, 1973), p. 534.

20. Kenneth Vaux, "Religious Hope and Technological Planning," in *To Create A Different Future,* ed. Kenneth Vaux (New York: Friendship Press, 1972), pp. 111, 120.

21. *New York Times,* December 20, 1973, p. 26 C; *Houston Chronicle,* December 21, 1973.

22. *Newsweek,* January 7, 1974, p. 49, January 14, 1974, p. 55; *Wall Street Journal,* December 26, 1973.

23. *Newsweek,* December 31, 1973, p. 35.

24. *New York Review,* December 13, 1973, p. 39.

25. Adapted, in part, from my critical review, "Theological Belief and Sociological Inquiry," *Journal of Religion,* 53 (April, 1973), 228–238, which treats Roger Mehl, *The Sociology of Protestantism,* tr. James H. Farley (Philadelphia: Westminster Press, 1970).

26. Bernard Malamud, *The Tenants* (New York: Pocket Books, 1972), p. 91.

27. Theodore H. White, *The Making of the President* 1972 (New York: Bantam Books, 1973), pp. 192–94.

28. KTRK, Houston, December 27, 1973, 7–8 p.m.

29. Thomas Thompson, *Hearts* (Greenwich, Conn.: Fawcett Crest, 1971), p. 220.

30. Thomas Jefferson, *Life and Selected Writings,* ed. Adrienne Koch and William Peden (New York: Modern Library, 1944), p. 491.

31. Jørgen Randers, "Global Limitations and Human Responsibility," in *To Creat A Different Future,* ed. Kenneth Vaux (New York: Friendship Press, 1972), pp. 30–32.

32. *Houston Chronicle,* October 13, 1973.

33. Jay and Heather Ogilvy, "Communes and the Reconstruction of Reality," in *The Family, Communes, and Utopian Societies* (New York: Harper & Row Torchbooks, 1972), pp. 88–96, 99.

34. Letter from Robert Reiss, Arlington, Virginia, July 26, 1972; Roszak, *Where the Wasteland Ends,* p. 387.

35. *Houston Chronicle,* December 16, 1973.

36. Paul Wohl in *Christian Science Monitor,* December 31, 1973.

37. *Houston Chronicle,* December 30, 1973.

38. Mayeroff, *On Caring,* p. 42.

39. *Christian Century,* July 4, 1973, p. 728.

40. Richard L. Merritt, *Symbols of American Community* 1735–1775 (New Haven: Yale University Press, 1966), pp. 184, 126.

41. Jefferson, *Life and Selected Writings,* p. 418.